NORTHERN COMFORT

FALL AND **WINTER RECIPES** FROM
ADIRONDACK LIFE

ISBN 978-0-922595-39-6

PUBLISHED BY ADIRONDACK LIFE, INC.
The Brick Church
12961 NYS Route 9N, Jay, NY 12941
www.adirondacklife.com

NORTHERN COMFORT
FALL AND WINTER RECIPES FROM ADIRONDACK LIFE
Editor Annette Nielsen
Designer Kelly Hofschneider
Copy editors Lisa Bramen, Niki Kourofsky, Annie Stoltie
Cover illustrator Peter Seward

WITH A FEW EXCEPTIONS, RECIPES IN THIS BOOK WERE PREVIOUSLY PUBLISHED IN ADIRONDACK LIFE MAGAZINE.
10 9 8 7 6 5 4 3 2 1

TABLE *of* CONTENTS

⇥ BEVERAGES ⇤

Adirondack fall brings stunning color to the landscape, regardless of your water's edge or woodland vista. Cool weather calls for warming drinks, like forager tea or mulled cider with citrus notes. Long winter nights mean more time for contemplation or creating a special brew drawing on local ingredients, from hops and herbs to melted snow.

SOOTHING TEA
Jane Desotelle, Chateaugay, New York
•----------•

There are more than 100 plants in the Adirondacks that can be used for herbal tea. Leaves from shrubs, stalks, even conifer needles can be steeped in hot water, yielding all kinds of health benefits.

Before trying a new wild fruit, root or shoot, always look it up in at least two field guides. (You might ask for these in your local library: *Edible Wild Plants* by Oliver Perry Medsger, Collier Books, 1974, and Lee Allen Peterson's *A Field Guide to Edible Wild Plants of Eastern and Central North America*, Houghton Mifflin Harcourt, 1999.) Whenever sampling a new edible, consume small quantities in case you have an allergy or it causes an upset stomach. This tea is said to relieve a hangover and settle nerves.

2 parts catnip
1 part wild thyme
½ part mint
½ part hops

Dry all the ingredients. You can hang bunches from the rafters of a room with good air circulation or place leaves on clean window screens in a sunny spot for several days. Gently crush and blend ingredients by hand and keep in a covered jar in a cupboard. Use about a teaspoon per cup of boiling water and steep 5 to 10 minutes. Strain and serve. —2002 ANNUAL GUIDE TO THE GREAT OUTDOORS

SNOW GODDESS PORTER
Katie Nightingale, North River, New York

• - - - - - - - - - - •

Geologist Katie Nightingale and her husband, Jake Haker, carry on the Adirondack tradition of growing hops and brewing beer at their home in North River. Although harvested in August and September, the buds can be frozen for making beer throughout the winter season, as the couple does for its annual party to appease the gods and goddesses of snow, in December.

This beer recipe requires basic brewing knowledge and equipment such as a carboy, airlock, beverage thermometer and bottle capper. A good handbook is *The Complete Joy of Home Brewing* by Charlie Papazian (Collins Living, 2003).

¾ **pound black patent malt**
¾ **pound crystal malt**
6⅔ **pounds amber malt extract syrup**
1½ **pounds dry amber malt extract**
3 **ounces hearty hops (bittering)**
1 **ounce hearty hops (aroma)**
1 **package English ale yeast**
¾ **cup corn sugar or dry malt extract**

Place crushed black patent and crystal malt in fresh water and steep at 155° for 30 minutes. Remove spent grains and add malt extracts and 3 ounces of hearty hops. Boil for 1 hour, drinking a home brew while you wait. Add 1 ounce hops for last 5 minutes of boil. Cool wort and pitch yeast. Ferment 10 to 14 days. (Check your favorite beer guide for fermentation instructions.) Bottle using corn sugar or dry malt ex-

tract. The porter is drinkable a week or so after bottling, but even sooner if kegged and force carbonated.

Note: This hearty brew goes nicely with sharp cheddar cheese soup or venison stew. Serve cool, not cold, for best flavor. —2008 COLLECTORS ISSUE

POWDERHORN PUNCH
Former Adirondack Life editors

•----------•

Before heading off on your next winter climb, mix the following ingredients in a large punch bowl to enjoy on your return. After two glasses, the pains of the climb will long be forgotten.

1 quart dark rum
1 quart good brandy
1 wine glass (6 ounce) apricot brandy
3 wine glasses (a little over two cups) simple syrup
1 quart melted snow
6 cinnamon sticks
2 oranges, sliced (with peel)
2 limes, sliced (with peel)
Sprinkling of cloves

To make simple syrup combine 2 cups sugar with 1 cup water in a medium saucepan. Stir over medium heat until sugar is completely dissolved. Remove from heat and allow to cool. Store in refrigerator in a sterilized jar.

Mix ingredients and set on the back porch to chill (or store in refrigerator) for up to 24 hours. You can also heat it over medium-low heat (do not boil), serving warm in a mug with a cinnamon stick. —WINTER 1972

HOT CITRUS TODDY
Carolyn Jabs, Mohawk, New York

• - - - - - - - - - - •

Use your woodstove to make this tangy, nonalcoholic warmer. The author suggests that many of the best beverage recipes benefit from simmering for an entire afternoon.

1 quart cider
2 cups orange juice
2 cups lemonade
½ cup sugar
⅓ cup molasses
1 lemon
6 cloves
1 stick cinnamon

Place all ingredients in a large saucepan. Stir until sugar dissolves. Poke half a dozen whole cloves into a lemon and float it on the punch along with a stick of cinnamon. Simmer as long as you like.

You can add a splash of rum to each mug of punch. —DECEMBER 1980

⊰ ACCOMPANIMENTS ⊱

Each regional cuisine has its signature condiments, such as
Louisiana's Tabasco, New Mexico's endless variations on salsa or
distinctive barbecue sauces from Memphis to Kansas City. In
the Adirondacks pantry jars echo our wild surroundings, using
rose hips or hawthorn fruit, and maple syrup adds the perfect
north-woods touch to venison snacks and relishes.

WARM FROM A NORTHERN KITCHEN

ADIRONDACK APPLE LEATHER
Elaine Priest, Eagle Bay, New York

•----------•

A wonderful way to preserve the season's bounty, apple leather takes little effort and makes a healthful snack. The recipe's author says that she doesn't even need an oven to make the fruit leather. "Living in the North Country, we usually have a woodstove burning, and I put some kind of flame-tamer between the cookie sheet and stove surface."

6–8 McIntosh apples
Pam cooking spray

Spray Pam on a nonstick cookie sheet or jelly-roll pan with raised edges. Peel and core apples and run through blender until they are the consistency of runny applesauce. Spread blended apples on cookie sheet and place on a moderately warm surface to dry, or bake about 45 minutes at 275°, checking frequently. When dry, tear or cut into strips and eat. —2003 COLLECTORS ISSUE

MAPLE VENISON JERKY
Annette Nielsen, Salem, New York

• - - - - - - - - - •

This recipe can be made in your oven, as long as the temperature can be set at 150º (or lower). The jerky can also be made in a food dehydrator following equipment instructions.

2½ pounds venison, cut into approximately ¼-inch-thick strips
⅓ cup Worcestershire sauce
⅓ cup maple syrup
⅓ cup apple cider vinegar

Mix liquid ingredients in a bowl. Place strips of venison in a glass baking pan and add liquid. Marinate in refrigerator, covered, for 12 to 24 hours.

Preheat oven to 150º. Using a roasting pan and rack, place the strips of meat over the rack, allowing the pan to catch the drippings.

Bake for about 6 hours in oven or until the jerky is dry but flexible. Check periodically to make certain the heat doesn't char the venison. Store in a sealed container in a cool, dry place. —2003 COLLECTORS ISSUE

PEMMICAN
Former Adirondack Life editors

•----------•

Authentic pemmican is made from jerky and various dried fruits that are sometimes hard to come by. This recipe utilizes readily available ingredients. YIELD: ABOUT 1 CUP.

2½-ounce jar of dried beef
¾ cup raisins
¾ cup peanuts or pecans
1 tablespoon honey
2 tablespoons peanut butter

Spread dried beef on baking pan and place in low (150º to 200º) oven for 20 minutes, turning once. Air-dry in a well-ventilated spot for an additional 24 hours, then run through meat grinder twice with raisins.

Thoroughly crush nuts in a coffee grinder or food processor to almost a powder and add to raisins and beef. Warm honey briefly and mix with peanut butter, then blend all ingredients. Stored in the refrigerator, this mixture will keep for an extended period of time. When eaten in small pinches as a trail snack, pemmican is nourishing yet will not cause excessive thirst. —SUMMER 1975

CRANBERRY-APPLE-ORANGE RELISH

Kenneth Wilson, Panama, New York

• - - - - - - - - - - •

Wild cranberries—found in many Adirondack ponds and lakes—have the color of autumn and the tang of the season's early frosts. This is a favorite accompaniment for holiday gatherings, or as a bright side dish for any meal with roasted fowl or game. YIELD: ABOUT 2 PINTS.

1 pound (approximately 4 cups) wild or cultivated cranberries

2 apples, peeled, cored and quartered

2 oranges, seeded and quartered (peel can remain if you prefer the extra citrus flavor)

1 lemon, peeled, seeded and quartered

2 cups sugar

Place all fruit in a food processor; chop for a few seconds to get desired consistency. Stir in 2 cups sugar (more or less, to taste). Chill for at least an hour. Can be prepared a day in advance and refrigerated for up to a month. —OCTOBER 1977

AUTUMN JAMS AND JELLIES
Elizabeth Folwell, Blue Mountain Lake, New York

•----------•

The hips, haws and berries of fall—astringent, peculiarly textured and not at all tasty in their natural state—are underappreciated, except perhaps for their decorative properties. But with a little simmering, sweetening and straining, this abundant Adirondack harvest produces delicious, tangy toppings with woodsy aromas.

HIGHBUSH CRANBERRY JELLY:

Highbush cranberries ripen mid-September through October and grow in garnet clusters on small trees. Look along roadsides or the edges of old fields to find the shrubs; highbush leaves are three-lobed and proportioned like a maple leaf.

YIELD: 6–8 HALF-PINT JARS.

Approximately 5 pounds highbush cranberries
Sugar

Wash the clusters of berries thoroughly, removing all the twigs and leaves. Open a window: the smell of simmering highbush berries is quite powerful. Place the fruit in a large enamel pot with water to cover and simmer gently, breaking open the berries with a wooden spoon—they'll "pop" audibly.

After 45 minutes to an hour of simmering and stirring, force the pulp through a sieve with the back of a wooden spoon or put it through a food mill. This will take care of any detritus you may have missed and separate out the seeds. (Each berry contains a single, surprisingly large disk-shape seed almost the diameter of an M&M.) Discard the seeds.

Measure the pulp. For each cup of cranberries add 1 cup of sugar. Bring to a boil for 5 minutes. Pack in sterile jars and seal. Note that highbush cranberries have plenty of natural pectin, so there's no need to add gelling agents.

Serve this jelly on bread, pancakes, muffins or biscuits, or as a condiment for roast turkey, pork or chicken. Thinned a bit with port wine, the jelly makes an excellent glaze for duck or Cornish hen.

ROSE HIP–APPLE BUTTER:

Rose hips are plentiful throughout the North Country and easy to recognize. You can find gone-to-wild and native rose bushes along abandoned fields and old foundations; the burnt-orange, ball-shape hips are more visible after the leaves die back in the fall. Rose hips are edible all year, but their texture and flavor are best after the first hard frost. From these flowery fruits you can make syrup for ice cream or pancakes, vitamin-rich tea, perfumy dessert wine, or jelly, as well as the following rose hip–apple butter. YIELD: 1 HALF-PINT JAR FOR EVERY CUP OF COOKED, SWEETENED PULP.

Rose hips
Apple cider
Sugar
Apples
Cinnamon
Nutmeg
Vanilla

Wearing long sleeves and gloves, gather firm (not squishy) hips that are unmarked and uniform in color, avoiding ones with black spots or tiny holes bored by larvae. (Soaking the hips in salt water for 10 minutes or so flushes out any bugs or worms.) Rinse well. Pull off the dried rose petals. This reveals lots of furry grayish seeds, which are supposed to be a good source of vitamin E. (The seeds will be removed when the pulp is strained.) The fruits are very high in vitamin C.

Put the rose hips in an enamel pan and cover with a scant amount of apple cider. Simmer gently for 1 to 1½ hours or until the rose hips are very soft. Strain out the seeds using a wooden spoon and sieve or a food mill. For every cup of rose pulp add 1 cup of sugar; 1 peeled, seeded, chopped apple; ½ teaspoon cinnamon; a tiny pinch of nutmeg; and ½ teaspoon vanilla extract.

Simmer slowly until the mixture thickens; stir occasionally. The butter is done when a spoon dragged through it leaves a trail that takes a moment to fill back in. Put in sterilized jars and seal.

Serve rose hip–apple butter on homemade buttermilk biscuits or on dark bread spread with a thin layer of cream cheese. It's also quite good dished up warm on vanilla ice cream.

MOUNTAIN-ASH JELLY:

Mountain-ash berries are an unmistakable and locally common fall fruit. One tree can supply all that you'll need for a batch of jelly, with the end result being a smoky, wild-flavored accompaniment for game, ham, goose or turkey. It's savory, like chutney, rather than a sweet spread for breakfast. In Scotland, the berries are called rowans, and rowan jelly is traditionally served alongside venison. YIELD: 8–10 HALF-PINT JARS.

Approximately 5 pounds mountain-ash berries
2–3 pounds tart, juicy apples (a mixture of wild and crab apples is fine)

Remove the stalks from the berries and quarter the apples (there is no need to peel or seed the apples). Place all ingredients in an enamel pan and barely cover with water. Simmer about an hour or until all the fruit is very soft. Scoop into a clean jelly bag and allow the mixture to drip overnight into a scrupulously clean glass container.

Measure the juice and add 1 cup of sugar to each cup and a quarter of juice. Bring the mixture to a hard boil, and keep it boiling until it reaches the setting point, about 220°. Test by placing a drop of the liquid on a saucer that's been chilled in the freezer; when the jelly sets up in a smooth blob rather than a shapeless, runny streak, it's done. (This jelly does not set as hard as most.) You can also use a jelly thermometer to test for doneness.

ADIRONDACK FOREST PRESERVES:
This Adirondack autumn jelly depends on the ingredients, but expect a spunky, flavorful spread that will, on a long winter's night, bring back memories of gleaming fall days.
YIELD: 1 HALF-PINT JAR FOR EVERY CUP OF COOKED, SWEETENED PULP.

Clear-skinned red or yellow hawthorns
Rose hips
Highbush cranberries
Mountain-ash berries
Wild and crab apples
Maple syrup
Apple cider
Sugar

Collect several cups of clean red or yellow hawthorns (being mindful of the long,

sharp spikes) and add an equal measure of rose hips, some highbush cranberries and a handful of mountain-ash berries. Add in 2 or 3 cups of coarsely chopped wild and crab apples. Barely cover with ½ cup of maple syrup and some tart cider. Simmer the mixture for an hour, stirring occasionally. To separate out the seeds, force the pulp through a sieve or food mill. Measure the pulp, and add a cup of white sugar for every cup of fruit puree. Bring to a boil, ladle into sterilized jars and seal. —OCTOBER 1992

MAPLE-CRANBERRY RELISH
Nikki Norman, Casselberry, Florida

• - - - - - - - - - - •

This take on the traditional cranberry relish will be a welcome addition to your holiday repertoire. Shallots and black pepper add a sophisticated spin. SERVES 8.

2 cups raw cranberries, rinsed
2 cups water
1 cup maple syrup
¼ teaspoon salt
2 shallots, finely chopped
1 tablespoon freshly ground black pepper

In a medium saucepan combine cranberries and water. Cover and cook over medium-high heat until all the cranberries have burst, approximately 10 minutes. Remove from heat and add maple syrup, salt, shallots and black pepper. Return to heat and simmer over low heat for 20 minutes, stirring frequently. Serve as a condiment with turkey, grilled chicken or baked ham. Keeps well for 2 to 3 weeks in refrigerator. —APRIL 2002

⊰ BREADS ⊱

Baking—using a wood cookstove or conventional oven—
defines the coming-inside seasons. Breads from the Adirondack
repertoire are hearty, relying on honey and molasses for sweetness, and adding herbs or orange peel to offer slices that only
need butter for the perfect fireside companion.

GRANDMA BROWN'S NUT BREAD

Bessie Malbone Marshall Brown, Lake Placid, New York
Submitted by Elvera Smith, Batavia, New York

• - - - - - - - - - •

This quick bread appeared in ADIRONDACK LIFE when the magazine solicited readers' favorite recipes. Brown was born in Wilmington, lived most of her life in Lake Placid and was Smith's grandmother. Smith noted that the recipe is easy, and that her grandmother was a "good, plain cook who often fried her own home-cured salt pork." YIELD: 1 LOAF.

1 egg
1 cup milk
1 cup sugar
3 cups flour
3 teaspoons baking powder
1 cup nutmeats, chopped
Pinch of salt

Preheat oven to 350°. In a medium bowl, lightly whisk egg and milk, set aside. In another bowl, sift together sugar, flour, baking powder and salt. Combine all ingredients and add the chopped nuts.

Pour into a greased baking pan or loaf pan and allow to rise for 30 minutes. Bake in a preheated oven for 1 hour, or until a toothpick inserted in the center of the bread comes out clean. —WINTER 1976

ORANGE RYE BREAD

Mary Heim, Garnet Hill Lodge, North River, New York

•----------•

YIELD: 2 LOAVES.

2¾ cups warm water
2 packages active dry yeast
½ cup firmly packed dark brown sugar
3 tablespoons softened butter or margarine
4 teaspoons salt
3 tablespoons grated orange peel
⅓ cup dark molasses
3¾ cups unsifted rye flour
5½ to 6½ cups unsifted white flour

Measure warm water into large, warm bowl. Sprinkle in yeast; stir until dissolved. Stir in salt, sugar, butter, orange peel, molasses and rye flour. Beat until thoroughly blended. Stir in enough white flour to make stiff dough. Turn out onto lightly floured board; knead until smooth and elastic, about 10 to 12 minutes.

Place in greased bowl, turning to grease top. Cover; let rise in warm place, until doubled in bulk, about 1 hour. Punch dough down; divide in half. Roll each half to a 14-by-9-inch rectangle. Shape into loaves by tucking long sides underneath. Place in 2 greased 9-by-5-by-3-inch loaf pans. Cover; let rise in warm place until doubled in bulk, a little over an hour.

Bake on lowest rack at 350° about 40 to 45 minutes or until done. Bread should sound hollow when thumped by your index finger. Remove from pans and cool on wire racks. —DECEMBER 1986

CORNBREAD
Agnes Spranz, Au Sable Forks, New York.
• - - - - - - - - - •

This recipe represents a mainstay of the old lumber camps, along with the corn chowder on page 34. Substituting maple syrup for white sugar makes a richer, more authentic flavor. SERVES 6–8.

1 cup yellow cornmeal
1 cup sifted all-purpose flour
¼ cup sugar (or ¼ cup maple syrup and decrease milk by 2 tablespoons)
4 teaspoons baking powder
½ teaspoon salt
1 egg
1 cup milk
¼ cup shortening, softened

Preheat oven to 425º. Sift together cornmeal, flour, sugar, baking powder and salt into a medium bowl. Add egg, milk, syrup (if substituting for sugar) and shortening. Beat with wooden spoon until smooth. Bake in a greased 8-inch-square pan for 20 to 25 minutes. —FEBRUARY 1977

BLUE RIBBON HERB BREAD

•----------•

When the temperature dips, it's comforting to have bread baking. This recipe by writer Mary Ann Evans makes bread for your household as well as a loaf or two for the neighbors. YIELD: 4 LOAVES.

4 tablespoons yeast
5½ cups lukewarm water
2 eggs
¾ cup vegetable oil
½ cup honey or molasses
4 teaspoons salt
8 cups whole-wheat flour
8 cups unbleached white flour
1 tablespoon dried dill
1 tablespoon dried thyme
1 tablespoon dried basil
2 teaspoons onion powder

Combine yeast, 1 cup of warm water and a pinch of salt and sugar and place in a warm, draft-free location until foamy.

In a large bowl, beat eggs, oil, honey or molasses, salt, yeast mixture, and 4½ cups lukewarm water. Add dill, thyme, basil, onion powder and whole-wheat flour. Mix well, gradually adding unbleached white flour. Knead 5 minutes. Place in oiled bowl, cover with a damp cloth, and let rise on warming shelf for 1 hour.

Remove dough from bowl and punch down. Divide into 4 loaves. Place in greased

8- or 9-inch loaf pans. Lightly oil tops, cover with a damp cloth, and let rise until doubled in size.

Bake at 375° for about 30 to 40 minutes or until tops sound hollow when tapped. Cap loosely with foil if tops begin to brown too quickly. Turning the pans after the first 10 minutes will ensure a more even browning. —DECEMBER 1985

GRANDMA'S DONUTS
Former Adirondack Life editors

• - - - - - - - - - - •

Here is a recipe for homemade donuts that is guaranteed not to fail, but be sure that you make enough, as they have a strange way of disappearing. YIELD: 10–12.

⅔ cup sugar
1 egg
4 tablespoons shortening
1 cup buttermilk
½ teaspoon baking soda
1 teaspoon vanilla
½ teaspoon salt
½ teaspoon nutmeg
2 cups flour
1 teaspoon baking powder

Cream together sugar, eggs and shortening. Thoroughly mix baking soda with buttermilk and add to egg mixture. Add vanilla to remaining ingredients, mix and combine with egg mixture.

Roll out dough to ¼-inch thickness on a lightly floured board. Cut with a donut press (you can also use a glass dipped lightly in flour, followed by a smaller cookie cutter to remove the donut "hole").

Fry the donuts in a heavy skillet, using approximately 3 inches of vegetable oil or melted shortening. Heat the oil to 375º. Slide the donuts into the fat (be careful not to crowd) and cook approximately 1½ to 2 minutes per side until golden brown.

(From the first batch, cut into one of the donuts to make certain that you are gauging doneness correctly.) Remove the donuts with tongs or a slotted spoon; place on paper towels to cool. When cooled, dust with sugar and/or cinnamon, if desired.

Best eaten immediately, though donuts will remain moist for a couple of days stored in a sealed container at room temperature. —FALL 1971

APPLE MUFFINS
Former Adirondack Life editors

• - - - - - - - - - - •

These country-style apple muffins make fine companions to bacon and eggs. YIELD: AP-PROXIMATELY 15 MUFFINS.

1 egg
4 tablespoons shortening, melted
½ cup sugar
2 cups flour
⅛ teaspoon nutmeg
4 teaspoons baking powder
½ teaspoon cinnamon
½ teaspoon salt
1 cup milk
2 medium apples, peeled, cored and coarsely chopped
For topping, 3 teaspoons sugar mixed with ½ teaspoon cinnamon

Preheat oven to 375º. Whip egg until blended; add sugar and melted shortening. Sift dry ingredients together. Add apples to egg mixture. Fold in dry ingredients alternately with milk until batter is moist. Do not beat or stir. Batter will be very soft and sticky.

  Fill greased muffin cups about ⅔ full. Sprinkle tops with sugar-cinnamon mixture. Bake 20 minutes at 375º. Muffins are best when warm but also tasty at room temperature. —FALL 1976

⇥ SOUPS & SALADS ⇤

Soups take center stage as fall arrives. Farm markets and gardens across the North Country overflow with potatoes and winter squash; the freezer yields homegrown sweet corn for chowder; the larder offers dry peas for the mainstay of Yankee and French-Canadian cooks, pea soup. Salads capitalize on the last hardy greens as well as cider and maple syrup, providing regional accents in dressings.

END-OF-SEASON GREENS WITH MAPLE-GLAZED ALMONDS, GOAT CHEESE AND MAPLE-BALSAMIC VINAIGRETTE
Patsy Jamieson, Burlington, Vermont

•----------•

An opener to a sturdy fall feast, Thanksgiving or holiday meal should be light and re-freshing. This salad of greens topped with local goat cheese and slivers of beet fits the bill. SERVES 8.

MAPLE-BALSAMIC VINAIGRETTE:
¼ cup extra-virgin olive oil
¼ cup finely chopped shallots (2 medium)
3 tablespoons balsamic vinegar
1 tablespoon pure maple syrup
2 teaspoons Dijon mustard
½ teaspoon salt, or to taste
Freshly ground pepper, to taste

Whisk all dressing ingredients in a medium bowl or shake in a jar with a tight-fit-ting lid. You can prepare the vinaigrette up to 2 days before serving and store in an airtight container in refrigerator.

GLAZED ALMONDS:
2 teaspoons olive or vegetable oil
2 teaspoons pure maple syrup
½ cup sliced almonds (2 ounces)

Preheat oven to 350º. Grease a small baking dish. Stir oil and maple syrup in a small bowl. Add almonds and toss to coat. Transfer to the greased baking dish and bake, stirring from time to time, until golden, 10 to 12 minutes. Let cool completely.

Prepare glazed almonds up to 2 days ahead and store in an airtight container at room temperature.

SALAD:
16 cups mesclun greens (10 ounces), washed and dried
1 cup crumbled goat cheese (4 ounces)
½ cup julienned or finely grated peeled raw beet (1 small)

Just before serving, put greens in a large salad bowl. Add dressing and toss to coat well. Top greens with glazed almonds, goat cheese and julienned beet.

—DECEMBER 2007

CHEF ERIC'S CIDER VINAIGRETTE
Eric Rottner, Tupper Lake, New York

•----------•

Rottner, former chef of the Wawbeek, a beautiful rustic lodge demolished in 2008, notes that fall cider is easy to source from any number of apple growers in the North Country. YIELD: ABOUT 3 CUPS.

2 eggs
½ cup powdered sugar
2 tablespoons Dijon mustard
1 teaspoon celery seeds
¼ teaspoon white pepper, ground
Salt, to taste
2–2½ cups peanut or sunflower oil
2 cups apple cider, boiled down to 1 cup

In blender, mix eggs, mustard, sugar and spices. Slowly drizzle in oil. As mixture thickens, add cider reduction, a little at a time, until all is incorporated. Keep refrigerated and use within a few days. —2003 COLLECTORS ISSUE

DAVID'S CHANTERELLE BISQUE
Caroline Seligman, Saratoga Springs, New York

•----------•

One of the benefits of a wet summer is an abundance of chanterelles in the fall. Although found in upscale markets, a knowledgeable forager can identify these lovely golden-yellow and orange specimens in an uncluttered autumn forest. Consult your favorite field guide for positive identification. SERVES 4.

½ pound chanterelles, cleaned and chopped into ½-inch pieces
4 tablespoons butter
1 tablespoon flour
2½ cups chicken broth or vegetable stock
Salt and pepper
Dashes of nutmeg and Tabasco
1 quart milk
1 tablespoon dry sherry

Save a few whole mushroom caps to slice and sauté for a garnish. In a large pan, melt butter and sauté onions over medium-high heat until transparent. Add the mushrooms and cook until soft. Sprinkle flour over the vegetables and stir for a couple of minutes. Gradually add the stock, then salt, pepper, nutmeg and Tabasco. Simmer 20 minutes over low heat. Puree, if desired, for a smooth texture, using an immersible blender. Add milk and sherry, heat (do not boil) and serve hot with sautéed caps as garnish.

Note: If using dried mushrooms, approximately 1 ounce of dried equals about 8 ounces of fresh. Reconstitute dried mushrooms per package directions. Save the soaking liquid, strain and substitute for part of the broth. —OCTOBER 1988

CORN CHOWDER
Dot Madden, Madden's Country Store, Jay, New York

•----------•

This hearty soup is perfect for lunch or a simple supper served with the recipe for corn-bread on page 22. Making the chowder with local sweet corn that you have blanched and frozen creates a more flavorful dish. SERVES 6–8.

1 piece fat salt pork (approximately 1-by-3 inches)
1 onion, thinly sliced
4 potatoes, cut in cubes
2 cups water
Salt and pepper, to taste
2 cups fresh corn (cut from the cob, canned, or frozen)
1 quart milk

Cut pork into small pieces and fry it in a pan over low heat. Add onion and cook for 5 minutes. Strain fat into a saucepan. Add the potatoes and 2 cups boiling water to the fat and cook until the potatoes are soft. Add the milk and corn. Heat to boiling. Season with salt and freshly ground pepper. —FEBRUARY 1977

PEA SOUP

Carolyn Jabs, Mohawk, New York

• - - - - - - - - - •

Although this recipe comes from a larger piece on woodstove cookery, it can be easily adapted for stove-top cooking. Substituting yellow peas for green split peas turns this Yankee staple into a French-Canadian dish. SERVES 6–8.

1 pound split peas (dried)
1 ham bone
2 stalks celery, chopped
2 carrots, chopped
1 onion, chopped
¼ teaspoon thyme
1 bay leaf
2 teaspoons salt
¼ teaspoon pepper, or to taste

Before breakfast, rinse and drain 1 pound of split peas and place in a large soup kettle with two quarts of water and bring to a boil. Remove from the fire (or from stove burner) and let peas soak while you eat breakfast.

Add ham bone, celery, carrots, onion, herbs, salt and pepper. Let the pot simmer while you do the morning chores. At noon, remove the bay leaf and the ham bone. Slice the meat off the bone, dice and return the meat to the soup. —DECEMBER 1980

SWISS POTATO SOUP
Rene Plattner, Rene's Mountain View House
Chestertown, New York

• - - - - - - - - - - •

Chef Rene Plattner operated his restaurant for more than a decade outside Chester-town, serving dishes from his native Switzerland. Venison, pork and spaetzle were pop-ular with the winter crowd.

If you don't have duck stock, substitute a rich beef or chicken broth. This is a quick and easy soup to have after a day out snowshoeing or skiing. SERVES 6.

½ onion, coarsely chopped
2 leeks or 6 scallions, coarsely chopped, including some green stalk
4 cloves garlic, minced
2 tablespoons butter
1 pound raw or cooked potatoes, peeled and coarsely chopped
3 cups duck stock
½ cup heavy cream
¾ cup grated Swiss or Gruyère cheese
Salt and freshly ground pepper, to taste

Melt butter in a large saucepan and sauté onions, leeks and garlic until golden, about 3 minutes. Add potatoes and stock. Bring to a boil, reduce heat and simmer 30 minutes. Cool, then puree in a blender or food processor fitted with a steel blade.

Strain pureed mixture back into saucepan. Add cream, return to stove and bring to a boil, then reduce heat. Taste for seasoning, and add salt and pepper, if needed. Just before serving, sprinkle with grated cheese. —JUNE 1999

VENISON SOUP

Bill Smith, Colton, New York

•----------•

For "Track Soup" writer Linda Batt sought out expert Adirondack cooks, folklorists and hunters for traditional Adirondack game recipes. Here's one by Bill Smith, a singer and storyteller. SERVES 8.

3–5 pounds venison bones with some meat still attached

3 stalks celery

2 medium onions, peeled and sliced in half

1 quart tomatoes

1 pound cooked elbow macaroni or ditalini

In a medium stockpot boil bones with celery stalks and onions for 3 to 4 hours. The meat will fall off the bones. Retrieve the meat from the stockpot and set aside.

Remove the bones. Skim the broth of foam and fat and add a quart of canned tomatoes for every quart of broth (estimate). Add cooked pasta and place meat back in stockpot. —DECEMBER 1997

VEGETABLE-BEEF SOUP
Beverly Fickbohm, Cranberry Lake, New York

• - - - - - - - - - - •

Soups and stews made on the woodstove fill the house with lovely aromas and offer great meals without using fossil fuels. Beverly Fickbohm wrote a collection of recipes using woodstoves rather than conventional ranges, and this is a classic winter bowl. SERVES 6 OR MORE.

1 meaty beef shank
2 medium onions, chopped
1 package or 2–3 cups frozen green peas
1½ cups fresh or canned green beans
1 cup celery, thinly sliced
1½ cups sliced carrots
1 small can corn
3–4 medium potatoes, pared and cubed
1 large can or 3–4 cups tomatoes
Salt and pepper, to taste

Place 1½ to 2 quarts cold water over shank in a large soup kettle over medium heat. (On a woodstove, use a trivet to regulate your heat.) Add all or any combination of the vegetables and simmer several hours.

Remove the beef shank. Cut meat from bone and return the pieces to the kettle; add salt and pepper, to taste. —FEBRUARY 1987

MAPLE–BUTTERNUT SQUASH SOUP
Deborah Ludke, Scotia, New York

•----------•

This creamy soup includes favorite flavors—savory and slightly sweet. Roasting the squash provides extra taste through caramelization. SERVES 4.

1 large butternut squash, about 2 pounds
1 14-ounce can chicken broth
½ cup maple syrup
1 cup half-and-half
Salt and pepper, to taste
½ cup sour cream
Chives, chopped (approximately ¼ cup)
2 tablespoons cream

Roast, peel and mash squash. Place squash in soup pot and add chicken broth and maple syrup. Cook 15 minutes until flavors meld. Cool briefly, puree in blender in batches; return to pot. Add half-and-half, salt and pepper. Simmer a few minutes more; do not boil.

Pour into soup bowls. Beat cream and sour cream. Swirl 1 or 2 tablespoons over top of soup and garnish with a sprinkling of chopped chives. —APRIL 2002

⊰ SIDE DISHES ⊱

If Adirondack food is roots cuisine, take "roots" literally here.
Beets, parsnips, potatoes, celeriac, onions and leeks thrive in our
challenging climate and make elegant sides for cold-weather
meals. These recipes also stand alone for delicious vegetarian
entrées. Aged local cheese enhances many casseroles; apples
add tartness and texture.

POTATO-PARSNIP GRATIN

Chef Robert Breyette, Lake Placid, New York

• - - - - - - - - - - •

Slow cooking, comfort food and aromatic root vegetables are the inspiration for this side dish created by Chef Robert Breyette (former Lake Placid Lodge chef; today chef/co-owner of Lake Placid's Caribbean Cowboy). Although you can make this without the prosciutto, it kicks the layering of flavors up a notch. SERVES 4–6.

1 teaspoon butter
1 clove garlic, peeled and halved
4 medium Yukon Gold or russet potatoes, peeled and sliced ⅛-inch thick
4 medium parsnips, peeled and sliced ⅛-inch thick
6 shallots, peeled, sliced and sautéed in 1 tablespoon butter until golden
1 quart heavy cream
Pinch of freshly grated nutmeg
Kosher salt and freshly ground pepper, to taste
¼ pound prosciutto or good-quality ham, sliced

Preheat oven to 350º. Butter a deep baking dish, sprinkle with a little salt and rub the garlic halves over bottom and sides.

In a large bowl, combine the potatoes, parsnips, sautéed shallots, cream and seasonings; mix well. Place half the potato mixture in the dish, patting it into place. Layer the prosciutto slices over the mixture, then add the remaining potatoes and cream. Cover with buttered foil to prevent burning.

Bake 1½ to 2 hours, until a knife inserted into the potatoes comes out clean. Remove foil and run under the broiler for a few minutes to brown. —APRIL 1999

BRAISED RED CABBAGE WITH APPLES
Peter Benoit, Queensbury, New York

• - - - - - - - - - •

This recipe uses primary ingredients that can be easily found in the North Country.
SERVES 6.

4 slices bacon, diced
1 medium yellow onion, minced
1 medium head red cabbage, coarsely chopped
2 tablespoons sugar
2 cups apples, peeled, cored and diced (preferably Northern Spy)
1 quart chicken stock (canned chicken broth may be used as a substitute)
Salt and pepper, to taste

In a large skillet, slowly sauté onion with bacon until bacon is slightly crisp. Add cabbage, sugar and stock and cover. Bring mixture to a boil over medium-high heat. Once boiling, reduce heat and simmer for 15 minutes. Add apples and cook another 5 minutes. Liquid should not evaporate or cabbage will burn. Drain any remaining liquid before serving. —2003 COLLECTORS ISSUE

SAUTÉED BRUSSELS SPROUTS WITH LEMON AND POPPY SEEDS
Patsy Jamieson, Burlington, Vermont
• - - - - - - - - - - •

When hearty brussels sprouts are shredded (simplified in a food processor) and quickly sautéed, they bear little resemblance to the strongly flavored ones you might remember from cafeteria steam tables. A finish of lemon zest and poppy seeds brightens the flavors. SERVES 8.

6 cups (approximately 1½ pounds) brussels sprouts, trimmed and cored
1 tablespoon vegetable oil
1 tablespoon butter
1 large onion, peeled and chopped (1½ cups)
1 cup reduced-sodium chicken broth or vegetable broth
2 teaspoons freshly grated lemon zest
3 tablespoons lemon juice
2 teaspoons poppy seeds
½ teaspoon salt, or to taste
Freshly ground pepper, to taste

Thinly slice brussels sprouts with a sharp knife or in a food processor fitted with a slicing disc. Heat oil and butter in a large non-stick skillet over medium-high heat. Add onion and cook, stirring often, until softened, 2 to 3 minutes. Add brussels sprouts and cook, stirring, for 2 minutes. Add broth, cover and cook until sprouts are crisp-tender, about 2 minutes. Stir in lemon zest, lemon juice, poppy seeds, salt and pepper. Serve hot. —DECEMBER 2007

BUTTERNUT SQUASH AND LEEK GRATIN
Patsy Jamieson, Burlington, Vermont

Instead of the standard mashed squash, try this crusty gratin as a great accompaniment to a Thanksgiving or holiday meal. It's also a lovely vegetarian entrée for fall. To make squash easier to peel, pierce it in several places, then microwave at high power for one to two minutes to soften skin. SERVES 8.

½ cup Japanese-style panko bread crumbs or fresh bread crumbs, divided
1 tablespoon olive or vegetable oil
2 large leeks (white and pale green parts only), cleaned (see tip) and thinly sliced (1¾ cups)
3 pounds butternut squash (1 large or 2 small), peeled, seeded and cut into ⅜-inch-thick slices (8 cups)
½ teaspoon salt
Freshly ground pepper, to taste
½ cup reduced-sodium chicken broth or vegetable broth
1 teaspoon butter, melted
1½ cups grated Adirondack Herdmaster or Couronne cheese from Clover Mead Farm, in Keeseville, or Swiss cheese (5 ounces)

Preheat oven to 400º. Grease an 11-by-7-inch or 12-by-8¼-inch shallow baking dish or gratin dish (2- to 2½-quart capacity). Sprinkle bottom with ¼ cup bread crumbs.

Heat oil in a skillet over medium-low heat. Add leeks and cook, stirring often, until tender, 4 to 6 minutes. (Add a little water if leeks start to scorch.) Set aside.

Spread half of the squash slices in prepared baking dish. Season with ¼ teaspoon salt, and pepper to taste. Spread leek mixture over squash. Top with remaining squash. Gently pour broth over squash. Season with remaining ¼ teaspoon salt, and pepper to taste. Cover baking dish with a greased sheet of aluminum foil. Bake until squash is almost tender, 30 to 40 minutes.

Sprinkle cheese over top of gratin. Mix remaining ¼ cup bread crumbs and butter in small bowl; sprinkle over cheese. Bake gratin, uncovered, until squash is tender and top is golden, 10 to 20 minutes.

Tip: Leeks often harbor dirt between layers so it's important to clean them thoroughly. Trim fuzzy root end and green stems. Use only the white and pale green portions. With a sharp knife, make several incisions at the stem end of leek to open it up like a fan. Soak leeks in a large bowl of water several minutes, then swish to dislodge dirt. Repeat until water runs clear and no trace of grit remains. —DECEMBER 2007

VIDALIA ONION AND APPLE CASSEROLE
Hannah Hanford, Peru, New York

•----------•

This dish is delicious with any pork recipe or steak on the grill. You can also add two to three large sliced portobello mushrooms to the sauté mixture and create a vegetarian entrée. SERVES 6.

½ cup butter
4 medium Vidalia onions, sliced thin
3 medium McIntosh apples, peeled, sliced ¼-inch thick
15–20 saltine crackers, crushed
1 can cream of mushroom soup, stirred
2 eggs, lightly beaten
½ cup milk
1½ cups Gruyère cheese, shredded
½ cup Parmesan cheese, shredded

Preheat oven to 350º. Melt butter in skillet and sauté onions over medium heat for 10 minutes, stirring frequently. Add sliced apples (plus optional mushrooms) and sauté until onions caramelize, 5 to 10 minutes more. Reserve 3 tablespoons of cracker crumbs for topping, and place the remaining crumbs over the bottom of a lightly greased 2-quart casserole dish.

Layer half of the soup, cheeses (save ¼ cup Gruyère for topping) and onion/apple mixture, then repeat. Combine eggs and milk and pour over onion mixture. Top with ¼ cup Gruyère and the remaining cracker crumbs.

Bake for 20 to 30 minutes, until bubbly and golden brown. —2003 COLLECTORS ISSUE

SCALLOPED POTATOES AND STUFFED BAKED POTATOES
The Tucker Family, Tucker Farms, Gabriels, New York
•----------•

Farming since 1865, the Tucker family works nearly 400 acres in seed and tablestock potatoes, as well as a variety of vegetables. The high-elevation plateaus where prevailing cool conditions limit pests are home to long-established tubers. The Tuckers sell their spuds to gardeners, commercial growers and to noted restaurants throughout the Adirondacks.

SCALLOPED POTATOES:
SERVES 6.
2 tablespoons flour
1½ teaspoons salt
⅛ teaspoon freshly ground pepper
2 pounds Adirondack blue potatoes, cut ⅛-inch thick (a favorite variety at the farmers' markets, flavorful, high in antioxidants—good all-purpose potato)
½ cup sharp cheddar cheese, shredded
2 tablespoons butter
1 cup whole milk
1 cup heavy cream or half-and-half
1 clove garlic, crushed (preferred) or ¼ teaspoon garlic powder
1 medium onion, diced

Preheat oven to 350º. Butter a 2-quart rectangular baking pan. In a separate bowl, combine milk, cream, cheese and garlic; in another, combine flour, salt, pepper and onion. Overlap half of the potato slices in pan and half of the onions. Sprinkle with

half the flour mixture and dot with remaining butter. Cover with last layer of potatoes and onions. Pour milk and cream mixture over top.

Cover with foil or pan lid and bake for 45 minutes at 350º. Reduce temperature to 325º and bake, uncovered, for another 45 minutes or until tinged with gold.

STUFFED BAKED POTATOES:

SERVES 6–12.

6 baking potatoes
3 tablespoons butter
1 can cream of broccoli soup
6 strips bacon, cooked and crumbled
¼ cup hot milk
6 tablespoons grated cheese of choice
Salt and pepper, to taste

Bake potatoes at 375º for 1 hour or until tender. Cut potatoes in half, scoop insides into a bowl; keep warm. Combine butter, salt, pepper, soup, milk, bacon crumbs and potato pulp thoroughly.

Stuff potato skins. Top with shredded cheese. Bake at 325º for 15 minutes.

—2006 COLLECTORS ISSUE

ROASTED POTATOES WITH ROOT VEGETABLES
Mark and Kristin Kimball, Essex Farm, Essex, New York

• — — — — — — — — •

In the Lake Champlain village of Essex, Mark and Kristin Kimball run Essex Farm, a community-supported agriculture operation. They have been growing potatoes since the mid-1990s. When dinnertime rolls around, they usually don't follow recipes, but "wing it," Mark says. This recipe preparation is best with firm roasting potatoes like fingerlings, and root vegetables. SERVES 4-6.

6–8 fingerling potatoes (red-skinned Red Thumbs or yellow LaRattes), quartered
2 medium beets, peeled and quartered
1 celery root, peeled and chopped into 1-inch pieces (optional)
1 small onion, chopped
3 cloves garlic, chopped
2 tablespoons rosemary, chopped
Salt and pepper, to taste
Lard, if available, or 2–3 tablespoons olive oil

Preheat oven to 400°. Toss all ingredients into a shallow baking dish. Dot the mixture with lard or toss all ingredients with olive oil to lightly cover. Bake for an hour, more or less, stirring and checking periodically. —2006 COLLECTORS ISSUE

MAPLE BARBECUE BEANS
Deborah Ludke, Scotia, New York

• - - - - - - - - - - •

In this recipe the layering of flavors is enhanced by the sweetness of the maple syrup playing off the bacon, onion and spice mixture. SERVES 6.

2 16-ounce cans Grandma Brown's Baked Beans
½ cup water
¼ cup olive oil
2 teaspoons finely chopped onion
½ cup maple syrup
¼ cup barbecue sauce
¾ teaspoon paprika
¼ teaspoon dry mustard
4 slices crisp cooked bacon

Preheat oven to 275°. Mix beans with all ingredients except bacon. Bake 1 hour covered with foil. Remove foil and top with bacon pieces; cook 30 minutes longer.

—APRIL 2002

MY FAMILY'S FAVORITE SWEET POTATOES
Be Denemark, Utica, New York

• - - - - - - - - - - •

This dish is reminiscent of family gatherings and holiday traditions. Maple syrup—rather than molasses or brown sugar—makes this a true North Country side dish. SERVES 8.

2 tablespoons butter or margarine
2 28-ounce cans sweet potatoes, drained and cut in chunks
1 14-ounce can pineapple chunks, drained and each cut in half
Salt and pepper, to taste
½ to ¾ cup orange juice concentrate (add ½ teaspoon orange zest if desired)
½ to ¾ cup maple syrup
1 Maraschino cherry for decoration

Preheat oven to 375º. Put small dabs of butter on bottom of 1½-quart casserole. Layer chunks of sweet potato, then a few chunks of pineapple. Lightly salt and pepper each layer. Add more dabs of butter on top, followed by another layer of potatoes and pineapples.

In a small saucepan, bring the orange juice and maple syrup to a boil and simmer for 5 to 8 minutes. Pour hot juice mixture over potatoes and pineapple and add more dabs of butter.

Decorate top with extra pineapple chunks. Bake for 15 minutes, covered; reduce heat to 350º, uncover and bake for another 30 minutes. Add cherry. —APRIL 2002

⊰ MAIN DISHES ⊱

Hunting season and harvest time bring authentic flavors to the Adirondack table. Main courses rely on game, meat and pasta, using techniques such as braising and roasting.

PASTA WITH CHANTERELLES
Caroline Seligman, Saratoga Springs, New York
• - - - - - - - - - - •

This recipe for a simple supper makes the easy transition between the lightness of summer eating and heartier fall fare. The chanterelles' golden color signals the change of seasons as the earthy aromas fill your kitchen. SERVES 4–6.

1 medium onion, chopped
1 pound chanterelles, cleaned and cut into small pieces
3 tablespoons butter
3 tablespoons olive oil
1 cup white wine
Pepper, sage and Tabasco, to taste
½ cup grated Parmesan cheese or more, to taste
1 pound linguine or fettuccine (preferably fresh)

Sauté onion in butter and oil in a large skillet over medium-high heat until transparent. Add mushrooms and cook until they give off most of their liquid.

In a medium-size saucepan, reduce the wine by half; add to the mushrooms and simmer briefly. Add freshly ground pepper, to taste, fresh or crumbled sage (approximately 1 teaspoon dried or 1 tablespoon chopped fresh) and a dash or two of Tabasco as the mushrooms simmer. Cook approximately 10 to 15 minutes. While sauce is cooking prepare pasta according to package directions.

Serve sauce over cooked and drained linguine or fettuccine. Sprinkle with Parmesan cheese.

Variation: Sauté ½ pound scallops in a little butter and add to the mushroom sauce the last 5 minutes.

Note: If you are unable to locate fresh chanterelles, 1 ounce dried mushrooms, reconstituted, is approximately equivalent to 8 ounces of fresh. Follow package instructions for reconstitution of dried mushrooms. —OCTOBER 1988

CHICKEN BREASTS WITH CHANTERELLE MUSHROOMS
AND WILD RICE

Mary Cuffe-Perez, Galway, New York
Adapted from Table for Two: Fresh Recipes for
Romantic Dining by Marianne Paquin

•----------•

Chanterelles offer up plenty of possibilities for mealtime—sautéed slowly in butter and parsley and served as an accompaniment, or used in a variety of meat and fish dishes. If you have gathered more chanterelles than you can use fresh, preserve the golden bounty by drying or freezing. This recipe will become a staple in your household, elegant enough for a dinner party, yet easy enough to whip up for a weeknight dinner. **SERVES** 2.

2 sprigs parsley
1 shallot
2 tablespoons cooked wild rice
2 boneless chicken breasts
¼ pound fresh chanterelles (10–12 mushrooms)
2 tablespoons butter
2 tablespoons olive oil
Salt and pepper, to taste

Wash, drain and chop the parsley. Peel and chop the shallot. Cook the wild rice according to package directions, making enough for 2 servings. Remove 2 tablespoons of the cooked rice for the stuffing mixture. Cover the remaining cooked wild rice and keep warm until ready to serve as an accompaniment for the entrée. Using a sharp knife, cut pockets in the chicken breasts, slicing lengthwise, almost halving them.

Wipe the mushrooms and slice into ¼-inch-thick pieces. Gently sauté in a large frying pan with shallots, parsley, rice and butter over medium heat for 3 minutes. Remove from pan and set aside.

Fill the chicken breast pockets with the mixture and secure with toothpicks. Heat the olive oil in a frying pan and cook the chicken, covered, for about 7 minutes on each side over medium-high heat. Serve with the reserved wild rice and a green salad.

—OCTOBER 2005

VENISON SAUTÉ OSWEGATCHIE

Jack Denton, The Arsenal Inn Restaurant, Elizabethtown, New York

• - - - - - - - - - - •

This is one of the very first recipes that appeared in ADIRONDACK LIFE during its inaugural year. Contributed by the owner of the landmark Arsenal Inn, the recipe pays homage to the wild country of the Oswegatchie River near Cranberry Lake. SERVES 2–4.

1–2 pounds venison steak or chops, 1½ inches thick
¼ pound butter
1 teaspoon Coleman's English dry mustard
1 serving spoon (or 2 tablespoons) *glace de viande* (see note)
1 teaspoon Lea and Perrins (Worcestershire) sauce
1 tablespoon cornstarch
1 ounce port or Burgundy wine
Salt and freshly ground black pepper, to taste

Salt and pepper the venison and place it in a hot saucepan in which the melted butter has sizzled. Cook 10 minutes, turning after 5 to 6 minutes, and remove from pan.

To the cooking butter and juice, add the dry mustard, *glace de viande*, Worcestershire sauce and cornstarch. Stir well, eliminating any lumps while simmering for 10 to 12 minutes over low heat. Next add the port or Burgundy wine while stirring. Simmer an additional 5 minutes.

Place steak in simmering gravy and leave for 5 minutes for rare, 7 minutes for medium, and 10 minutes for well done. Place venison on a platter. Strain gravy and pour hot over steak or chop. Garnish with chestnuts, wild-rice fritters and currant jelly.

Note: French for meat glaze, *glace de viande* is made by boiling meat juices until they are reduced to a thick syrup. It's used to add flavor and color to sauces, and can be purchased at the market, or made at home with your own meat juices and beef stock. (Combine drippings or juices from a venison or beef roast or steak with approximately 5 cups of beef stock. Place in a small stock pot over medium heat and simmer until it has reduced by about ¾, or when the stock is thick enough to coat the back of a spoon when dipped into the mixture. Although this process can take several hours, any remainder will store well in a jar, refrigerated, for up to two months.) —FALL 1970

LAMB SAUSAGES WITH TOMATO SAUCE

Sylvia Newman, Valley View Farm, Saranac, New York
Adapted from a recipe in World Food Greece by Susanna Tee

• - - - - - - - - - - •

A growing trend in the Adirondacks is raising excellent lamb, beef, pork, venison and rabbit sustainably. Sylvia Newman, of Valley View Farm, raises lambs and offered one of her favorite recipes using ground lamb, based on a Smyrna-inspired, cumin-infused dish. SERVES 4.

SAUSAGE:
1 pound lean, finely ground lamb
1 cup fresh unflavored bread crumbs
1 onion, finely chopped
3 garlic cloves, chopped
3 tablespoons finely chopped parsley
2 teaspoons ground cumin
Pinch of ground cinnamon
Salt and pepper, to taste
1 egg, beaten
2 tablespoons olive oil

TOMATO SAUCE:
1 pound, 12 ounces canned chopped tomatoes with juice
¼ teaspoon sugar
¼ cup olive oil
2 garlic cloves, crushed

½ teaspoon ground cumin
1 tablespoon chopped parsley
1 bay leaf
Salt and pepper, to taste

To make the sausages place ground lamb, bread crumbs, chopped onion, garlic, parsley, cumin, cinnamon, salt and pepper in a medium-size bowl and blend well. Stir in the beaten egg and knead the mixture for a few minutes, until it forms a paste. Allow to chill, covered, in the refrigerator for about 1 hour.

While the sausage is chilling, prepare the tomato sauce by placing all of the ingredients in a large saucepan (large enough to hold the sausages in a single layer). Bring to a low boil over medium-high heat and reduce, allowing to simmer for 30 minutes.

Form the lamb mixture into 12 equal-size sausage shapes, approximately 3 inches long. Heat the oil in a large skillet, add the sausages and sauté for 15 minutes, until browned on all sides. Using a slotted spoon transfer the sausages to the pan with the tomato sauce and simmer for an additional 15 to 20 minutes over medium heat. Serve hot with rice or pasta. —INSPIRED BY "BONE APPÉTIT," AUGUST 2008

COLA ROAST

Craig DuMond, Windy Knoll Farm, Ray Brook, New York

•----------•

Although this retro recipe could be prepared any time of year, its longer cooking time is perfect for cooler weather. Cola is traditionally used to tenderize meat, but also adds a nice balance to the hot and spicy sauces included below. SERVES 6–8.

1 teaspoon salt
½ teaspoon pepper
½ teaspoon garlic powder
4- to 5-pound beef roast
3 tablespoons vegetable oil
1½ cups cola-flavored beverage
12 ounces chili sauce
2 tablespoons Worcestershire sauce
1–3 teaspoons hot sauce, to taste

Combine salt, pepper and garlic powder; rub over surface of roast. Brown roast on all sides in vegetable oil in a Dutch oven. Place small wire rack under roast in Dutch oven; combine remaining ingredients and pour over roast. Bake uncovered at 325° for about 2½ hours or until tender. Remove roast and wire rack from Dutch oven and reduce remaining sauce on top of stove, thickening, if necessary, with a mixture of red wine and a little flour.

Serve with mashed potatoes, spooning sauce over potatoes and meat. —INSPIRED BY "BONE APPÉTIT," AUGUST 2008

BRAISED RABBIT
Heather Burk, Burky-B's Farm, Dickinson Center, New York

•----------•

Rabbit is becoming popular once again as another "other" white meat, high in protein and low in fat. Heather Burk raises rabbits on her farm, free-range fashion. She touts the simplicity of cooking a rabbit, as you'll see by her recipe below. SERVES 4.

1 whole 3-pound rabbit, cleaned and cut into 6 pieces
1-quart jar of tomato sauce or 1 bottle of Ken's (or similar style) Lemon and Pepper Marinade

Pat rabbit pieces dry, place in a baking pan and cover with marinade or tomato sauce. Cover baking dish with aluminum foil. Slow cook in a preheated 325° oven for 3½ hours. —INSPIRED BY "BONE APPÉTIT," AUGUST 2008

BRAISED RABBIT II
Annette Nielsen, Salem, New York
• – – – – – – – – – •

SERVES 4.

2 tablespoons olive oil, more if needed
4 ounces bacon, diced
1 whole rabbit, about 3 pounds, cleaned and cut into 6 pieces
Salt and pepper, to taste
1½ cups flour
1 green pepper, cleaned, ribs removed, and cut into 1-inch pieces
2 carrots, peeled and cut into 1-inch pieces
1 large onion, peeled and coarsely chopped
5 cloves garlic, chopped
1 bay leaf
2 teaspoons dried rosemary
2 teaspoons dried sage
1 teaspoon dried thyme
3 tablespoons tomato paste
1½ cups red wine
1 pint (2 cups) crushed tomatoes with sauce

One way to ensure a tender rabbit is to marinate it in a couple of cups of red wine for about 24 hours prior to cooking, covered and refrigerated.

Preheat oven to 350º. Heat olive oil in a large Dutch oven over medium-high heat. Sauté bacon until lightly crisp. Remove bacon from pan. Sprinkle rabbit with salt and pepper, dip in flour, shaking off any excess. Increase heat to high. Add rabbit, in batches if necessary, browning on all sides, a couple of minutes for each side. Remove rabbit from pan and reduce heat to medium-high. Add peppers, carrots, onions and garlic. Sauté until golden, approximately 2 minutes. Add herbs, tomatoes and tomato paste. Stir well to combine and cook 1 or 2 minutes. Add wine and stir well, scraping up any browned bits in the Dutch oven. Return the rabbit, bacon and any juices to Dutch oven, spooning some sauce over the rabbit. Cover and bake for about 1½ hours, until the rabbit is tender. Remove from oven and serve with sauce.

—INSPIRED BY "BONE APPÉTIT," AUGUST 2008

EGGPLANT AND SAUSAGE CASSEROLE
Elizabeth Folwell, Blue Mountain Lake, New York

• - - - - - - - - - - •

The Spear family at Yellow House Farm, in Upper Jay, formerly raised heritage-breed pigs and their ground pork provided the inspiration for this flavorful casserole. Great for bringing to a harvest gathering, it makes use of late-season eggplant, tomatoes and New York State cheddar cheese. Simple to prepare and a meal on its own—add a salad, a baguette and you've got supper. SERVES 4.

1 large eggplant, peeled and cubed
1 pound lean ground pork
2 cups tomato sauce, homemade or canned
1 (generous) cup grated New York State sharp cheddar cheese
1 cup bread crumbs
Salt and pepper, to taste

Preheat oven to 375º. Steam eggplant cubes in a basket until tender, about 10 minutes. Sauté ground pork in a frying pan until cooked through. Drain off any fat. Grease a covered 3-quart casserole dish. Mix the tomato sauce with the cooked ground pork. Place half the sausage, half the eggplant, half the bread crumbs and half the grated cheese in the casserole. Repeat layers.

Bake at 375º for 30 to 40 minutes covered, then remove cover to brown the cheese, approximately 5 to 10 minutes. —INSPIRED BY "BONE APPÉTIT," AUGUST 2008

VENISON STEW WITH CIDER AND BOURBON
Annette Nielsen, Salem, New York

• - - - - - - - - - - •

This dish is reminiscent of an Adirondack beef Bourguignon. Serve with string beans and buttered, parsleyed noodles. Biscuits or a baguette are handy to sop up gravy; finish the meal with baked apples with maple syrup and a dollop of *crème fraîche*. SERVES 6.

2½–3 pounds venison, cut into 1½-inch cubes
¼ cup flour
1 teaspoon salt
½ teaspoon black pepper
3 tablespoons olive oil or rendered chicken fat
2 large onions, diced
4 cloves garlic, minced
1 teaspoon fresh thyme, chopped
1 teaspoon fresh rosemary, chopped
1 cup tomato sauce
¼ cup bourbon
½ cup apple cider
½ cup beef broth

Mix flour, salt and pepper in a shallow bowl. Gently toss venison cubes in mixture. Set aside.

   Using a 12-inch enameled cast-iron skillet, heat oil or chicken fat until hot. Brown the cubed venison a few pieces at a time, and with a slotted spoon transfer to a bowl. Sauté the onions and garlic in the skillet over medium-high heat until soft-ened. Set aside.

Transfer the venison pieces to a flameproof casserole. In a small saucepan, heat the bourbon slightly. Pour over the venison and ignite with a match, shaking the casserole until the flames die out.

Add onions, garlic, herbs, tomato sauce, cider and broth. Cover and simmer over low heat for about 2 hours, checking the liquid throughout, adding more broth as needed. —2003 COLLECTORS ISSUE

SHOOTER'S SANDWICH
Diane Bielejec, Frankfort, New York
•----------•

On a weeklong trip for deer or a daylong hike for woodcock, the problem of what to eat is ever present. The standard fare of soggy sandwiches may suffice for a day or two, but soon the taste buds clamor for something more exciting. And here it is: a delicious, portable, sportsman's meal, like a meatloaf sandwich ready to go. And even if you have never shot anything but a game of pool, this is perfect for a picnic. SERVES 4–6.

1 loaf day-old French bread

HERBED BUTTER:
8 tablespoons (1 stick) melted butter
2 teaspoons dried thyme
2 teaspoons dried oregano
1 tablespoon minced parsley

STUFFING:
1¼ pounds ground round steak
1 teaspoon salt
½ teaspoon pepper
½ medium onion, diced
1 teaspoon prepared mustard (Dijon works well)
1 tablespoon ketchup
1 tablespoon Worcestershire sauce
1 beaten egg

½ cup bread crumbs (made from bread inside loaf)

Remove 2-inch-thick slice from each end of the bread and scoop out the inside, leaving a ¾-inch crust on all sides. Brush the inside of the loaf and the cut ends with the herbed butter.

Mix stuffing ingredients and pack into hollow loaf. Replace the bread ends and top, wrap loaf loosely in foil. Place on a baking sheet and bake at 350º for 1½ to 1¾ hours. Pack hot for room-temperature serving or cool for an easy-slicing cold treat. —FALL 1974

MEDALLIONS OF VENISON WITH CARAMELIZED APPLES AND CILANTRO

Douglas M. Petroski, Queensbury, New York

•----------•

SERVES 8.

8 venison tenderloin steaks, sliced 1-inch thick (approximately 3 pounds)
1 cup flour
1 teaspoon salt
½ teaspoon freshly ground black pepper
Pinch cayenne powder
1 teaspoon garlic powder
1 tablespoon paprika
1 tablespoon onion powder
½ white onion, diced
3 garlic cloves, thinly sliced
1½ cup apples, diced into small cubes
1 cup apple cider
Juice of ½ lemon
2 tablespoons soy sauce
Butter
Olive oil
¼ cup fresh cilantro, minced

Combine the dry ingredients in a small mixing bowl. Mix well with a fork. Place venison medallions between 2 sheets of plastic wrap and gently pound out to 1½ times original size. Dredge in the seasoned flour. Reserve.

Sauté onions, garlic and the diced apples in a skillet in 1 tablespoon butter and 1 tablespoon olive oil over medium heat. Reserve.

Sauté venison medallions in a large skillet over medium heat in the same amounts of butter and oil, turning frequently, about 4 minutes.

Transfer the venison to warm plates. Deglaze the skillet over medium-high heat with cider and lemon juice. Add the apple, onion and garlic mixture and the cilantro. Add the soy sauce and stir. When warm, pour over venison. —2003 COLLECTORS ISSUE

ALMOND-CRUSTED CHICKEN BREASTS WITH CIDER CREAM SAUCE
Hannah Hanford, Peru, New York

• ---------- •

This dish takes no time to prepare and, for a little effort, produces a sweet and savory main course. It's great with nutty rice pilaf and sautéed fall greens like Swiss chard. SERVES 4.

4 boneless chicken breasts, skinless, flattened
¼ cup flour, seasoned with salt and pepper
1 egg, beaten
1 cup sliced almonds
2–4 tablespoons olive oil
2 Cortland or Honeycrisp apples, cored and sliced into ¼-inch rings
2 cups apple cider
2 tablespoons Dijon mustard
1 cup heavy cream
Salt and freshly ground black pepper, to taste
⅛ teaspoon nutmeg

Heat oil in large nonstick skillet over medium heat. Dip the chicken breasts in the flour, then the egg, and finally the sliced almonds. (Pat the almonds to help them stick to the chicken.)

Sauté the chicken breasts until golden brown, turn and repeat. Place chicken on a rimmed baking sheet and bake at 325° for 5 to 10 minutes, until done. Meanwhile, add apple rings to skillet and sauté until crisp-tender (not mushy).

In a 2-quart saucepan, reduce the cider to ½ cup over medium-high heat. Whisk in the mustard and cream and reduce to about ¾ cup total liquid. Season with salt, pepper and nutmeg, and keep warm.

To serve, place a chicken breast on each plate, garnish with apple rings and sauce. —2003 COLLECTORS ISSUE

GROUSE MARSALA AND WOODCOCK SAUTÉ
Georgia Jones, Lake Placid, New York
• - - - - - - - - - - •

In some households, autumn brings days of grouse and woodcock. Each has a unique flavor that can be enhanced with herbs, wine and quick cooking.

Note that wild game should not be treated like domestic chicken because partridge and woodcock lack the fat layer found in even the youngest broilers. Skinning these small birds is much easier than plucking, and most cooks feel that they're best eaten fresh. If you plan to serve woodcock as a main course, a few very successful days of shooting are necessary to feed 4 people. SERVES 4.

GROUSE MARSALA:
8 split breasts of grouse
4 tablespoons flour
1 teaspoon salt (or to taste)
Freshly ground black pepper, to taste
6 tablespoons butter
1 tablespoon fresh chopped parsley
½ tablespoon lemon juice
¼ cup chicken broth
¼ cup Marsala wine

Dust the breasts with flour, salt and pepper. Brown in 3 tablespoons butter, 3 minutes per side.

Remove grouse to a hot platter. Add remaining butter, parsley, lemon juice, broth and Marsala to the pan and simmer over medium heat for 10 minutes more.

For a rare treat, serve this with fresh green beans garnished with lemon rind, some boiled potatoes and a nice red wine, like Bordeaux.

WOODCOCK SAUTÉ:
4 tablespoons butter
6 tablespoons chopped scallions
8 woodcock breasts
¼ cup red wine

Melt butter and lightly brown scallions. Add woodcock breasts and sauté 5 minutes over medium-high heat. Add wine and simmer 8 to 10 minutes longer.

Add wild rice, ratatouille, a tossed green salad and a light red Beaujolais to make a delightful dinner. —OCTOBER 1989

TURKEY PIE
Hopkinton Congregational Church, Hopkinton, New York

• – – – – – – – – – – •

For the Hopkinton Congregational Church's annual fund-raiser, which dates back to the late 1960s, churchwomen make 40 to 50 turkey pies every year, serving 150 people in the town hall on the second Saturday of September. SERVES 6.

2 cups Bisquick
⅔ cup whole milk
1 cup peas and diced carrots, cooked
2 cups diced turkey, cooked
About 2 cups turkey gravy, cooled
Salt, to taste
Flour (for dusting board, rolling pin and hands)

Preheat oven to 400°. Mix Bisquick and milk well. Flour a board, rolling pin and your hands. Divide the dough in two. Roll out half of the dough and slip it onto a pie plate with a spatula. (The secret of a fluffy crust is the dough must be sticky.)

Mix vegetables and meat in a bowl. Fill the pie with the mixture. Roll out the rest of the dough. Pour enough gravy to cover the filling. Put the top crust on and crimp the edges. Poke steam holes with a fork. Bake about 30 minutes, until lightly browned. Serve with additional gravy.

***Note*: Boil leftover turkey bones and giblets for stock to make gravy. Melt 2 tablespoons of butter or margarine for each cup of broth you have, add the same amount of flour as butter and stir over low heat, adding broth until it thickens. Cooling the gravy before adding it thickens it and prevents a soggy crust.** —OCTOBER 2007

SPIEDINI DI VITELLO

Adapted by Bill McKibben, Johnsburg, New York

•----------•

SERVES 2.

4 4-ounce top-round veal cutlets
3½ tablespoons extra-virgin olive oil
3 cloves minced garlic
10 sprigs Italian parsley
Freshly ground black pepper
2 tablespoons Locatelli Genuine Pecorino Romano
4 thin slices prosciutto
4 slices mild provolone
2 tablespoons olive oil
Round toothpicks

Pound veal cutlets between a couple of sheets of plastic wrap until very thin. Spread a mixture of the extra-virgin olive oil, garlic, Romano cheese and parsley evenly over the cutlets. Place one slice of prosciutto and provolone on each piece of veal.

Roll cutlets like a jelly roll and secure on both ends and the middle with toothpicks. Fry veal rolls in olive oil until browned all around. Remove toothpicks and serve with fresh vegetables. Can also be served with a Marsala wine sauce with mushrooms. —DECEMBER 1993

NORTH COUNTRY MAPLE WINGS
Elaine Priest, Eagle Bay, New York

• - - - - - - - - - - •

This recipe can turn out a nice appetizer or serve as the main event for a simple supper.
SERVES 4.

20–24 chicken wings, separated
Cooking oil
½ cup maple syrup
1 tablespoon vermouth
¾ teaspoon ground ginger
½ teaspoon garlic powder
¼ teaspoon Gravy Master (browning agent)
⅛ teaspoon black pepper
Dash Tabasco (optional)

In electric frypan or heavy skillet, brown chicken wings in oil, turning a couple of times until skin starts to turn golden. Mix remaining ingredients in a bowl, stirring well. Pour over browned wings. Cover and simmer for 1 hour. Uncover and simmer for 15 minutes more.

Note: An alternative method for cooking is to place wings on a baking sheet and bake at 375° for approximately 40 minutes, turning once halfway during cooking. If there are any leftovers, drain liquid from wings and store overnight in the refrigerator. (Extra sauce can be frozen for a later batch.) —APRIL 2002

PORK OR VENISON MARINADE
Barbara Wood, Malone, New York

•----------•

This is a nice twist on the classic rib marinade. If wild leeks or ramps aren't available, consider a mix of leeks and/or shallots to obtain a similar flavor. Wood's recipe works as an appetizer, and also as a marinade for pork tenderloin. The instructions call for a microwave oven as well as a Crockpot, but you can use your range top and oven. SERVES 2.

1 pound pork ribs or other meat
2 tablespoons mustard (Dijon, preferably)
2 tablespoons ketchup
2 tablespoons soy sauce
2 tablespoons garlic, chopped
¼ cup maple syrup
1 cup hot water
1 handful wild leeks, chopped (or regular leeks and/or shallots)
1 dash of Tabasco sauce
1 teaspoon freshly ground pepper

Bake ribs at 350° for 1 hour; drain off fat.

   Mix the wet and dry ingredients plus leeks or shallots and microwave covered for 5 minutes. (If not using a microwave, place in a saucepan and simmer for 5 minutes.) Pour marinade over ribs in a Crockpot and cook 3 to 4 hours on low until done. —APRIL 2002

FRIED SALT PORK AND CREAM GRAVY
Dot Madden, Madden's Country Store, Jay, New York

•----------•

Madden's store was next door to the brick church that now serves as ADIRONDACK LIFE's offices. The general store, which sold everything from kerosene-lamp chimneys to salt pork to wool socks, was demolished in the late 1990s. Here, this staple of pioneer kitchens is made into gravy that can be served over a baked potato, pork chops or even thick slabs of homemade bread. SERVES 4–6.

1 pound salt pork
Boiling water
½ cup cornmeal
2 tablespoons fat (or oil)
4 tablespoons flour
2 tablespoons fat from salt pork
2 cups milk

Have salt pork sliced ¼-inch thick. Pour boiling water over the meat in a medium saucepan and boil for approximately 15 minutes to render fat. Drain pieces of pork well and dip the slices in cornmeal.

Cool the cooking water until fat congeals on top. Spoon off 2 tablespoons for frying salt pork slices golden brown, about 15 minutes. Remove another 2 tablespoons of fat for gravy. Remainder can be refrigerated for another use. Discard water.

To make cream gravy, place fat in a frypan over medium heat. Add flour to melting fat, stirring constantly. Add milk gradually until thickened. Serve over pork chops or baked potatoes. Garnish with crunchy bits of fried salt pork. —FEBRUARY 1977

BEEF SURPRISE
Rena Baker, Willsboro, New York

•----------•

This old-time dish resembles a roulade, substituting potatoes as the filling. SERVES 6.

2 pounds ground beef
2 teaspoons salt
2 teaspoons onion juice
⅛ teaspoon pepper
2 tablespoons Worcestershire sauce
1 egg, slightly beaten
3 cups well-seasoned mashed potatoes

Preheat oven to 350°. In a medium-size bowl, season ground beef with salt, onion juice, pepper and Worcestershire sauce. Add beaten egg. Place meat on a piece of waxed paper and beat out to almost ¼-inch thickness. Form mashed potato into a roll 8 inches long and 4 inches across. Wrap meat around potato roll, overlap edges and press firmly. Remove waxed paper.

Bake in a lipped pan or shallow baking sheet for 45 minutes.

Note: **This freeform meatloaf can be shaped into small rolls, dipped in egg and bread crumbs and fried in deep fat.** —SPRING 1975

MARINATED VENISON BACKSTRAPS
Paul Gillette, Inlet, New York

•----------•

Paul Gillette, a chef at a hunting club, provided his suggestions for a tender venison backstrap with marinade that can be used for a barbecue or roast. This technique calls for a slow oven, resulting in tender but not rare venison; many prefer to cook game quickly, preserving a pink, juicy interior. SERVES 6–8.

2 venison backstraps (this is the meat running parallel to and on either side of spine, typically 3–4 pounds of meat)
6 cups olive oil
2 cups red wine vinegar
Fresh garlic in great quantity, minced and squeezed into the mix (at least ⅓ cup)
Generous portion of basil leaf (fresh, if possible—¼ cup loosely packed)
¼ cup fresh rosemary and thyme leaves combined
Salt and freshly ground pepper

Butterfly the 2 venison backstraps and spread meat open. Apply the marinade, cover and place in the refrigerator for at least a day and a half, turning the meat frequently.

Remove meat from marinade. Strain the herbs and place on the cut side of meat before tying. Use string (a number of 6- to 8-inch pieces) and roll the edges of the meat together and tie off every 3 to 4 inches. The roast should be cooked slowly to a medium interior temperature, either in the field, over open hardwood coals or on the backyard grill. To prepare in a conventional oven, cook in low heat (300°) until the internal temperature reaches between 150° and 160° for medium (depending on the thickness of the backstraps, approximately 30 to 45 minutes). —DECEMBER 1987

ROAST GOOSE
Roxie Hammond, Chateaugay, New York
• - - - - - - - - - •

Hammond was nearly 90 years old when her method for cooking goose appeared in
ADIRONDACK LIFE. She recalled watching her mother and grandmother processing
the geese by dry plucking (so that the feathers could be used for pillows and com-
forters) followed by washing the birds in mild soapsuds to open the pores and drain out
some of the fat. She recommended buttering the outside of the goose and drawing off
the fat that forms in the early stages of cooking. Hot water added to browned butter and
seasonings were used for basting—the trick being to get the bird well done, but not
dried out. SERVES 4–6.

1 goose, cleaned, rinsed and patted dry (typically 4–5 pounds, dressed)
1 apple
1 onion
2 tablespoons butter
3 sprigs fresh sage
Salt and pepper

**Preheat oven to 375º. Rub the skin of the goose with butter. Sprinkle salt and pepper
inside the goose cavity and on the exterior. Place onion, apple and sage sprigs in
goose cavity and position the goose, breast side up, on a rack set in a roasting pan.**
　**Tent the goose with aluminum foil and roast for an hour, basting the bird with the
pan juices every 10 to 15 minutes. After an hour uncover the bird and roast for approximately 1 hour longer.** —DECEMBER 1987

BAKED SALMON
Christine Fadden, Onchiota, New York

•----------•

Christine Fadden—who, with her late husband, Ray Fadden, founded the Six Nations Indian Museum, in Onchiota—grew up in the Akwesasne Mohawk Community, a member of the Turtle Clan of the Mohawks. She recalled eating salmon from the St. Lawrence River as a child. A traditional Iroquois method for salmon calls for wrapping fresh fish in peppermint leaves and cornhusks, adding salt, and covering fish with large slabs of tree bark. These are buried about eight inches deep in a bed of charcoal and left for two hours. Mrs. Fadden's own recipe for preparing salmon is adapted from a book of western cooking and uses vegetables available in any store. SERVES 6–8.

3–4 pound salmon, whole or large fillet
½ cup olive oil
2 tablespoons butter, melted
Salt and pepper
1 clove garlic, crushed
1 large onion, sliced in thirds
1 large tomato, sliced in thirds
1 green pepper, cored, seeded and membranes removed, sliced in thirds
½ cup sherry
2 teaspoons Worcestershire sauce

Preheat oven to 400º. Coat a large baking pan with the olive oil and add the melted butter. Place the whole salmon in the pan, season with salt and pepper and the crushed garlic. Top with onion, tomato and pepper slices. Add more seasoning to taste and cover the fish with parchment paper or aluminum foil.

Bake whole fish for 45 minutes, but for fillets cut the time in half. Remove parchment paper or aluminum foil. Mix together sherry and Worcestershire sauce; pour over fish. Bake uncovered until the fish is a rich golden brown. —DECEMBER 1987

VENISON KABOBS
Annette Nielsen, Salem, New York

• - - - - - - - - - - •

Whitetail-deer hunting in the Adirondack Park begins with archery in September, muzzle loaders in mid-October and rifle season in late October through early December. Create a venison-themed evening with kabobs, raclette, steaks and bundles. Substantial sprigs of rosemary can be used as the skewers, imparting flavor as the kabobs cook, or just use smaller rosemary sprigs as garnish for a festive platter. SERVES 4.

2 pounds venison, cut in 1½-inch cubes
1½ pounds shiitake mushrooms, stems removed
¼ cup olive oil
2 tablespoons freshly squeezed lemon juice
1 tablespoon rosemary, minced
4 cloves garlic, peeled and minced
Minced parsley for garnish

Combine the olive oil, lemon juice, rosemary and garlic in a ceramic bowl. Mix in venison cubes; cover and refrigerate for at least 1 hour. Turn on oven broiler or heat grill until quite hot.

Alternating venison cubes and mushrooms, place on small skewers (or rosemary sprigs) until both ingredients have been completely used. Brush each skewer with any additional marinade.

Place on medium-hot section of the grill or under the broiler, turning after 2 minutes and basting until all sides are golden brown. Remove kabobs and serve immediately. —2003 COLLECTORS ISSUE

VENISON RACLETTE
Annette Nielsen, Salem, New York

•----------•

Fondue was the communal culinary rage in the 1970s. Now we've returned to a centuries-old cooking style with cheese raclette—derived from the French word *racler*, meaning "to scrape"—a dish that comes from cowherds in the Swiss and French Alps. Raclette cheese was melted on hot rocks near a campfire. Today's electrified version uses a raclette machine—a two-level grill with separate pans and mini spatulas for the cheese—accomplishing the same job, but saving you the trouble of building a fire and heating rocks. SERVES 6–8.

2 pounds new potatoes (no larger than 2 inches in diameter)
2 pounds New York State cheddar cheese (or locally produced Saratoga Sunflower or Casino Jack cheese, or other artisanal, regional cheeses that can be thinly sliced or grated—see www.nyfarmcheese.org)
2 pounds cooked venison sausage, sliced into ½-inch-thick rounds
1 loaf peasant bread from Crown Point, Rock Hill or other artisan bakery, cut in 1-inch-thick slices
4 tablespoons melted butter

Fill a large stockpot with water and bring to boil over high heat. Add new potatoes and cook until tender, approximately 15 minutes. Drain and set aside. In medium bowls, place the grated or sliced cheese, sausages and potatoes, sliced in half.

Preheat the raclette grill. Brush melted butter on griddle (top portion of raclette) and fill individual cheese pans with a single layer of sliced or grated cheese. Cook on bottom layer of raclette until melted and bubbling. While cheese is cooking, place slices of venison sausage and potatoes on grill, cooking until golden. The cooking process on the raclette should take about 5 minutes.

Place sausage slices and potatoes on a plate, scraping melted cheese on top. Take a forkful of sausage or potato, scooping up some cheese, or eat them on bread as a rustic sandwich.

Note: If you are unable to find a raclette grill, you can substitute a couple of electric frypans for cooking the cheese on a medium-low temperature, cooking the meats and potatoes in a lightly greased skillet on the stove top. You can add dried jerky, sliced peppers, onions and mushrooms to grill. —2003 COLLECTORS ISSUE

VENISON STEW
Carolyn Jabs, Mohawk, New York

•----------•

This is an exceptional woodstove meal. The stew can also be prepared on a gas or electric range in a Dutch oven. SERVES 6.

3 pounds venison (or chuck roast), cut into 1-inch cubes
Flour
Salt and pepper
4 tablespoons olive oil (or rendered duck fat)
1 cup chopped onion
1½ cups red wine
1 cup water
1 tablespoon tomato paste
2 cloves garlic, chopped
1 tablespoon paprika
1 cup sour cream

Dredge meat cubes in flour seasoned with a little salt and pepper. In a cast-iron pot, brown the meat on all sides over medium-high heat for a few minutes. Set aside.

Sauté the chopped onions in the remaining oil (add more if needed) for a few minutes over medium-high heat. Stir together red wine, a cup of water, tomato paste and garlic, and add to the onions. Return the meat to the pot, sprinkle paprika over the stew and simmer until the meat is tender, at least 2 hours. Replenish the liquid with water as necessary. Just before serving, stir in a cup of sour cream. Spoon stew over cooked buttered noodles or spaetzle. —DECEMBER 1980

FRENCH-CANADIAN MEAT PIE
Mrs. John E. Delehanty, Tupper Lake, New York

•----------•

This *tourtière*—French-Canadian meat pie—is a hearty two-crust main course tradition-ally served around the holidays. Families in Tupper Lake and other communities had their own approaches, using potatoes, different spices and changing proportions of beef and pork, even substituting venison for the beef. SERVES 6.

¾ **pound coarsely ground beef**
¾ **pound coarsely ground pork**
3 medium onions, chopped
½ **teaspoon salt**
1 teaspoon pepper
½ **teaspoon sage**
1 double piecrust (see recipe on page 128)

Preheat oven to 375°. Mix all ingredients together. Add sufficient water to just cover and simmer in a medium frypan for an hour or until meat is tender. While simmer-ing, make a double piecrust shell using only ⅔ the amount of shortening normally required. Pour meat mixture into 9-inch pie shell, cover with top crust, and slit top to allow steam to escape. Bake for 45 minutes or until golden brown. Serve piping hot with dill pickles.

Note: **Meat mixture may be cooked a couple of days ahead, refrigerated, and ex-cess fat may be removed. These pies freeze nicely.** —WINTER 1976

TOURTIÈRE

Cecile Garso, Au Sable Forks, New York

•- - - - - - - - - - -•

The late Cecile Garso, grandmother of ADIRONDACK LIFE staffers Janine Sorrell and Joni Manning, was born and raised in the Trois-Rivières area of Quebec. She retained her Canadian citizenship along with many aspects of her French culture and language even after moving to Au Sable Forks in 1937. Garso served *tourtière* at Thanksgiving and Christmas feasts. YIELD: 4 PIES.

4 pounds ground pork
1 tablespoon salt
1 large onion, finely diced
½ teaspoon pepper
1 tablespoon allspice
8 potatoes, cooked, drained and mashed

Brown pork until pinkness is completely gone. Drain off any fat. Add onion, salt, pepper and allspice. Cover with water and simmer for 1 hour. Add mashed potato, stir well and cool. This makes filling for 4 9-inch pies, so make enough crust for 4 2-crust pies (see piecrust recipe on page 128). Bake pies at 400° for 40 to 45 minutes. Pies or filling can be made ahead and frozen. —DECEMBER 2008

GAME METHODS
Kay Kennedy, Hannawa Falls, New York; Sal Smith, Colton, New York; and Gus Hedlund, Canton, New York

• - - - - - - - - - - •

After a couple of misadventures in venison preparation, writer Linda Batt embarked on a quest to learn the key to cooking game, enlisting the help of folklorist Varick Chittenden, of the Traditional Arts in Upstate New York, in Canton. While researching cooking traditions for a public radio series, Chittenden had talked with old-time kitchen experts. He shared his interview tapes with Batt. The following methods were taken from those interviews.

Kay Kennedy
PHEASANT:
Take a pheasant, cover it with garlic and butter and wrap it in aluminum foil. Put some holes in the bottom to let the fat out. Cook in a slow oven until it's fork tender. Uncover it. Sprinkle it with sherry and put it back in the oven for a few minutes at a higher temperature to brown.

RABBIT:
Parboil the rabbit in a big kettle of water with a couple of teaspoons of baking soda, which will bring the residue from the rabbit up to the top. Then put it in clean water for another half hour. Fry it in an iron skillet with butter, salt, pepper, onions and green peppers. Or, once the meat is tender, you can roll it in cornflake crumbs and deep fry.

Sal Smith

CANNED VENISON:

Cut venison into 1-inch pieces. Pack a quart jar half full. Make sure the meat is tightly packed by pushing it down with a wooden spoon. Add a teaspoon of salt and then fill the quart jar up to the top. Screw on the lid and process for 90 minutes in a pressure canner. These jars supply the basic ingredient of many dishes.

VENISON STEW:

Open a jar of canned venison and pour the broth in a kettle. Add a quart of home-canned tomatoes. Then put in chopped onions, carrots and potatoes. Let the pot simmer until the vegetables are tender. Add the meat and thicken the stew with a little flour and water. Serve with biscuits.

VENISON STEAKS:

Steaks should be cut thin and fried in a hot cast-iron pan. Put in the meat, salt and pepper. Heap 3 or 4 chopped onions over the top and fry in butter. You can also add mushrooms and green peppers.

PARTRIDGE:

Sauté chopped onions, celery and apples in butter. When the vegetables and fruit are tender, add cubes of bread and Bell's Poultry Seasoning. Let the mixture stand for 20 minutes so the bread soaks up the moisture.

Put the dressing in a roasting pan. Add a split partridge per person and cover the entire pan with mashed potatoes. Put the top on the roasting pan and cook in a 300° oven for 2 hours. Test the partridge for tenderness using a fork. If the birds are done, uncover the pan and turn the oven up to 400°. Cook for another 10 minutes to brown the mashed potatoes.

Gus Hedlund

JERK VENISON:
Cut the venison into chunks and put salt and pepper on it. Wrap the meat in a deer hide and bury the hide in a swamp for 4 days. Start a charcoal fire and cover the coals with hemlock-bark chips. Smoke the meat all day.

VENISON STEW:
Coat 3 pounds of venison cut in 1-inch chunks with ¾ cup flour seasoned with salt and pepper. Melt 8 slices of diced salt pork in a pan and brown the venison in the drippings. Add the browned meat to 2 cups of water in a large kettle and simmer covered for an hour.

Melt 3 tablespoons of butter in a skillet and add 3 whole diced onions, 3 chopped celery stalks, 2 diced green peppers and 6 garlic cloves. Sauté until tender. Then add these vegetables and 5 cut carrots to the venison kettle. Simmer for another hour. In the last half hour, add 10 whole allspice berries, 4 tablespoons of Worcestershire sauce and ½ cup of red wine. —DECEMBER 1997

VENISON OSSO BUCO
Chef Mark Trietley, North River, New York

• - - - - - - - - - - •

High Winds Inn, at the original site of the Barton garnet mines, in North River, operated as an upscale lodge and restaurant for about a decade. The menu featured local fare, including High Winds' Chef Mark Trietley's North Country riff on an Italian kitchen's staple, a dish typically made with veal shanks and a gremolata (a mix of parsley garlic and lemon peel). The venison takes center stage here and chutney infuses the dish with hints of spices and mango. SERVES 4.

1 pound Anasazi or pinto beans
1 32-ounce jar Major Grey's Mango Chutney
2 large Spanish onions, medium dice
4 large venison shanks (cross-cut 1-inch-thick, if possible)
Salt and freshly ground black pepper
1 cup all-purpose flour for dredging
1 tablespoon ground cumin
1 teaspoon ground coriander
1 teaspoon ground nutmeg
2 tablespoons vegetable oil, more if needed
1 quart low-sodium chicken broth
1 quart low-sodium beef broth

Rinse beans well, place in a pot with ½ gallon of cold water and soak overnight. Change water several times. Drain beans, measure them, place in a saucepan and add double their volume of water, along with half the chutney, an onion and salt, to taste, and cook gently until tender, 1 to 2 hours. Drain and reserve.

While the beans are cooking, salt and pepper the shanks. In a heavy-bottomed pot, heat the oil until hot but not smoking. Mix flour with spices. Dredge the shanks in the seasoned flour; knock off excess, and brown slowly on all sides. Set aside.

Add the remaining onion and chutney plus all the broth to the pot, stirring to remove caramelized bits of meat and flour. Add the shanks (they should be covered by the broth) and bring to a boil. Reduce heat and simmer until fork tender, up to 2 hours. The broth should reduce considerably.

Add the drained beans, adjust seasoning and simmer until heated through. If the sauce is thin, mix 2 tablespoons cornstarch with 2 tablespoons cold water, stir until smooth, then add. Heat until thickened. Serve with seasonal vegetables and lots of crusty bread. —APRIL 1999

BAKED WILD TURKEY AND TA-HA-WUS TURKEY STUFFING
Former Adirondack Life editors
• - - - - - - - - - - •

Tahawus, also known as Adirondac, is now a ghost town near the trailhead to Henderson Lake. The community was originally a mining settlement founded in the 1820s. The name of this dish is misleading, since wild turkeys were not common in this part of the Adirondacks until the 1990s. If you're lucky enough to have a wild turkey, follow Western adventure author Zane Grey's instructions below for cooking the bird in a campfire or fireplace. SERVES 8.

BAKED WILD TURKEY:
Let the dressed turkey hang for a night or 2 in the frosty air. Disjoint, turn in well-seasoned flour and brown in bacon fat in Dutch oven. Add a little water, cover oven and heap with hot coals, banking down so that coals will hold the heat. For a young bird, cook about 3 hours. Larger ones should be cooked longer, and coals kept hot.

TA-HA-WUS TURKEY STUFFING:
Giblets, cooked in water in saucepan for 20–30 minutes
1 cup butter
½ cup chopped onion
½ cup diced celery
3 cups ¼-inch cubes day-old bread
3 cups coarsely crumbled cornbread
1 cup browned, crumbled sausage
1½ cups walnut meats, chopped
¾ teaspoon salt

¼ teaspoon pepper
1 teaspoon sage
2 teaspoons summer savory
2 teaspoons minced parsley
½ cup dry white wine

Sauté cooked, drained and chopped giblets with onion and celery in butter gently
for 5 to 10 minutes. Add bread, cornbread, sausage, walnuts and seasonings and
mix lightly but thoroughly. Gradually add enough wine to moisten dressing nicely.
Makes dressing to stuff a 10-pound bird.

Note: If you prefer to cook the dressing separately from the turkey (a good idea if
your bird is roasting in a Dutch oven piled with coals), place in a lightly greased
casserole dish and cover. Bake at 350º for 1½ hours. Remove cover for final 30 minutes of cooking. —WINTER 1971

BRAISED YELLOW HOUSE FARM PORK SHOULDER
Julie Robards, Upper Jay, New York.

• - - - - - - - - - - •

In 2003 John and Martha Spear purchased the Torrance Homestead, in Upper Jay, and renamed it Yellow House Farm. They pasture-raised their heritage-breed pigs— Gloucestershire Old Spots, Tamworths and Hampshire crosses. Julie Robards is an avid cook and friend of the Spears. Robards says that braising one of their pork shoulders gets terrific results, as the meat is so flavorful and tender it will fall off the bone. This method is also how she makes pork chops and beef roast or short ribs, yielding savory meat and rich, flavorful gravy. This dish works great in a Dutch oven. SERVES 6.

Pork shoulder or roast (approximately 2½–3 pounds)
1 stick (¼ pound) butter
Salt and pepper
Cold water
Cornstarch for thickening gravy

Heat the pan over medium-high heat. Add a stick of butter and allow to melt, being careful not to let it brown or burn. Tip the pan to evenly coat the entire bottom. When the butter is sizzling hot add the pork roast and begin searing. It is important in browning the meat to let it sear until it no longer sticks to the pan. Turn with tongs to brown on all surfaces. When meat is entirely browned on all sides, season liberally with salt and pepper and add enough cold water to almost cover the roast.

Reduce heat to low and cover tightly. Let meat slowly simmer for 5 hours, check-ing often to be sure liquid level does not reduce completely. Skim off fat. Add water as needed. Eventually the meat will become tender enough to remove the bone and excess fat. Just before serving, remove meat to a large platter. Cover with foil and place in a warm oven. Set aside the liquid to cool a bit.

GRAVY:
Skim all remaining fat from the liquid by using ice cubes. (Add a tray full of ice cubes and the fat will solidify around them. Skim off the solid fat that forms with a slotted spoon, adding more ice cubes as needed. They won't dilute the gravy.) Once the fat has been removed, return the pan to medium-high heat and bring to a simmering boil. Dissolve ¼ to ½ cup of cornstarch in an equal amount of cold water and blend or whisk until it has the consistency of milk. Slowly add to simmering liquid, stirring constantly until gravy reaches desired thickness.

Note: Julie and her husband Terry, of Terry Robards' Wines & Spirits, Ltd., in Lake Placid, pair this dish with a food-friendly Pinot Noir or Burgundy, or a hearty French Gigondas from the Rhône Valley. (Gigondas is a neighbor of Châteauneuf du Pape, making the same types of wines at a fraction of the cost.) —INSPIRED BY "BONE APPÉTIT," AUGUST 2008

⇥ DESSERTS ⇤

The finale to any regional meal should leave behind memories of place, flavors and aromas that evoke the setting long after guests have pushed back from the table. Apples, cranberries, pumpkin and maple underlie cakes, fritters and even crème brûlée. Raisins have been an Adirondack kitchen staple for generations, and North Country cooks love chocolate too, in everything from bread pudding to pie.

PYE OF GREEN APPLES

John Gorman, Black Bear Lodge, Pleasant Valley, New York

• - - - - - - - - - - •

Celebrate fall and the first apples of the season with a recipe that appeared in the inaugural issue of ADIRONDACK LIFE. This dish was adapted from a 16th-century British recipe. SERVES 6–8.

3–4 pounds of early apples
Cinnamon and sugar

Peel and core the apples. Slice ⅛-inch thick. You'll need approximately 7 cups for a 9-inch pie.

Shingle slices in layers in pan lined with dough (see below) until pan is filled. Sprinkle each layer with sugar and cinnamon to taste and dot with small pats of butter.

Note: Later in the season, as apples ripen and sweeten, lemon juice may be sprinkled on layers to add tartness.

PASTRY:
2 cups sifted all-purpose flour
1 teaspoon salt, sifted again with flour
⅔ cup shortening
Water

Preheat oven to 450°. Add flour with salt to shortening little by little, cutting in with a knife until the flour and shortening particles are the size of large peas. Keep ingredients cool and handle the dough as little as possible. Add cold water a teaspoon at a time and mix with a fork until all dough is dampened.

Gather dough into 2 balls (⅔ of the dough for the bottom of a 9-inch pan and ⅓ of the dough for the top). Roll lightly with rolling pin on a flour-dusted board to keep from sticking. Place dough in pan and fill as directed above. Top dough should be rolled out about 1 inch larger than diameter of pie tin. Seal edges by crimping with fork tines and puncture holes on top in several places with fork.

Place in hot oven at 450° for 10 minutes; reduce heat to 350° for 45 minutes longer. —WINTER 1970

APPLE KUCHEN
Mrs. William H. Andrews, Albany, New York

• - - - - - - - - - •

According to notes in the Fall 1973 issue of ADIRONDACK LIFE, "apple kuchen is both simple to prepare and delightfully tasty (so easy that a culinarily catastrophic editor could prepare it and so good that a staff of three could devour it in one hour)."

¼ cup butter
1 cup sugar
2 eggs
¾ cup milk
2 cups flour
2 teaspoons baking powder
1 teaspoon vanilla
¼ teaspoon salt
¼ cup nutmeats
6 apples, peeled, cored and sliced
2 tablespoons sugar and cinnamon (mixed)
¼ cup shredded coconut
¼ cup raisins
1 tablespoon powdered sugar

In a mixing bowl, cream together butter and sugar. Add eggs, one at a time, and beat well. Stir in milk and sifted flour, baking powder, vanilla and salt. Beat about 3 minutes.

Preheat oven to 375º. Place half the batter in well-greased pan (9-inch-square or

9-by-13-inch for thinner kuchen). Cover with apples, raisins, nuts and half the coconut. Sprinkle with cinnamon-and-sugar mixture, then pour on remaining batter
(since it is a bit thick, dab it on smoothly with a fork or rubber spatula). Sprinkle
with rest of coconut and bake until brown, approximately 30 minutes. Dust with
powdered sugar. —FALL 1973

POACHED PEARS
Annette Nielsen, Salem, New York

• - - - - - - - - - •

Another fruit of the harvest season, pears are as versatile as apples. Bartlett, Bosc and even small Asian pears can be found in modern North Country orchards. SERVES 4.

4 small pears (not overly ripe)
1½ cups port or red wine
¾ cup sugar
1½ cups water
1 lemon, sliced
4–5 whole cloves
Stick of cinnamon
Parchment paper

Peel pears, leaving stem on; cut a thin slice from the bottom so they can stand on their own. Place in a bowl of water with fresh lemon juice to prevent from turning brown.

In a medium saucepan, bring port or wine, water and sugar to a boil. Turn heat to medium-low and add lemon, cinnamon stick, cloves and pears. Cover the pan with parchment paper cut to the diameter of the saucepan; cover with lid and simmer until very tender, at least 20 minutes.

Remove the pears to a bowl and continue to cook the sauce until it is reduced by half and becomes syrupy. Strain the syrup over the pears and refrigerate overnight. Serve the chilled pears whole, on a plate with a dollop of whipped cream and/or mascarpone. Drizzle a couple of spoonfuls of reduced sauce over each pear. —INSPIRED BY "ESPRIT DE CORE," 2003 COLLECTORS ISSUE

APPLESAUCE CAKE
Carolyn Schaefer, Keene, New York

• - - - - - - - - - •

Carolyn Schaefer, the proprietor of Skyline Outfitters, in Keene, from the 1960s through the early 1980s, says this local favorite dates back to "when people came in by wagon and buckboard and stayed in hotels and boardinghouses. The cook during those days was Eliza Sullivan, of Keene." SERVES 6–8.

1 cup raisins
1 cup hot, fresh applesauce
½ cup butter or shortening
1 cup sugar
1½ cups flour
1 teaspoon baking soda
½ teaspoon salt
½ teaspoon cinnamon
¼ teaspoon nutmeg
¼ teaspoon ground cloves
½ cup chopped walnuts

Preheat oven to 350º.

APPLESAUCE:
Peel, core and slice 4 to 5 medium-size apples. Place in large, heavy saucepan with ½ cup cider or water. Simmer over medium-low heat until apples soften, checking to make certain enough liquid remains to prevent the apples from scorching.

CAKE:

Soak raisins in hot water for approximately 15 minutes, set aside. Pour hot apple-sauce over shortening and mix thoroughly. Sift together dry ingredients and add to applesauce and shortening mixture.

Drain raisins and add to cake batter. Pour into a greased 9-inch-square pan, top with chopped walnuts, and bake for 45 minutes. Serve warm.

Variation: Substitute ½ cup brown sugar for ½ cup white sugar. Top with additional hot applesauce. —FALL 1975

CRANBERRY PIE

Kenneth A. Wilson, Panama, New York

• - - - - - - - - - - •

Wild cranberries are a resource that renews annually, but pick with respect, without damage to plants. If your harvest from a favorite bog leaves you with more than you can use in cranberry-apple relish (see page 11) or cranberry sauce, try this recipe for cranberry pie. SERVES 8.

⅓ **cup water**
2 cups sugar
2 tablespoons all-purpose flour
¼ teaspoon salt
1 pound fresh cranberries (approximately 4 cups)
Favorite piecrust, unbaked

Preheat oven to 425º. In a large saucepan over medium heat, mix water, sugar, flour and salt, stirring until all ingredients have dissolved. Add 1 pound fresh cranberries. Boil gently until the cranberry skins burst. Cool slightly; pour into a dough-lined 9-inch pie tin, cover with slats of pie dough or a full upper crust, crimping the edges to secure. Use a fork to create a few steam holes and bake for 30 minutes or until the crust is golden brown. —OCTOBER 1977

PUMPKIN COOKIES
Jean Kratz, Westport, New York.
•----------•

Pumpkin (and winter squash) puree can be made into more than pies or side dishes for the harvest table. YIELD: APPROXIMATELY 3 DOZEN.

1 cup shortening
1 cup sugar
1 cup cooked pumpkin (see note)
1 egg
2 cups flour
1 teaspoon baking soda
1 teaspoon cinnamon
½ teaspoon salt
1 cup raisins (or substitute ½ cup chopped walnuts for ½ cup raisins)

Preheat oven to 375º. In a mixing bowl blend shortening, sugar and pumpkin. Add egg and mix well. Add remaining ingredients and drop in rounded teaspoons onto ungreased cookie sheet. Bake for 10 to 12 minutes.

Note: To process pumpkin pulp take an 8- to 10-pound sugar or pie pumpkin, split in half (seeds and stringy parts removed) and place the 2 pieces face down on a baking sheet with a little water. Cover lightly with foil and bake in a 350º oven for approximately 45 minutes to 1 hour. The pumpkin is fully cooked after it becomes soft to the touch. Remove from the oven and allow to cool. Scoop out the flesh and place in a food processor for a few seconds, until smooth. An 8- to 10-pound pumpkin should yield 7 to 8 cups of pumpkin puree. Extra can be frozen in ziplock bags. —FALL 1972

MAPLE-PUMPKIN CRÈME BRÛLÉE
Annette Nielsen, Salem, New York
•----------•

This classic dessert with a twist is easily prepared with leftover pumpkin puree. SERVES 8.

8 egg yolks
2 cups heavy cream
1 cup pumpkin puree
½ cup maple syrup
¼ cup sugar
2 teaspoons vanilla
½ teaspoon grated nutmeg
½ teaspoon cinnamon
½ cup sugar (for topping)

Preheat oven to 350°. In a large mixing bowl, whisk together egg yolks, cream, pumpkin puree, maple syrup, ¼ cup sugar, vanilla and spices until very smooth. Divide the mixture among 8 6-ounce ramekins or ovenproof cups.

Place cups in shallow baking pan; pour in enough boiling water to rise halfway up the sides of the ramekins. Bake until the edges look set and the center of the custard still moves slightly, about 35 minutes. Remove the ramekins from water and refrigerate until cold, 2 to 3 hours. Bring to room temperature; sprinkle the tops with sugar and broil 6 inches from broiler or use a pastry torch until caramelized, about 2 minutes; refrigerate again until chilled, about 1 hour. Can be prepared up to 6 hours ahead. Keep refrigerated until serving. —INSPIRED BY "SWEETENING THE POT," APRIL 2002

SWEDISH APPLE PIE
Jack Smolik, Johnstown, New York
• - - - - - - - - - •

This classic doesn't use a traditional piecrust, minimizing preparation time. SERVES 6.

1 extra-large egg
¾ cup sugar
2 cups apples (Cortland, Macoun or very early McIntosh; approximately 2 apples)
½ cup flour (sifted)
1 teaspoon baking powder
1 tablespoon vanilla
Dash salt
½ cup walnuts, chopped (optional)
½ cup raisins (optional)
Sweetened whipped cream (1 cup heavy cream, 3 tablespoons sugar, 1 teaspoon
vanilla, combined and beaten until very stiff)

Preheat oven to 350°. Grease a 10-inch Pyrex pie dish with butter. Core and dice
apples, leaving skins on. Beat egg, sugar, vanilla and salt until frothy.
   Stir in apples. Sift flour and baking powder into batter. Gently but thoroughly
blend entire mixture. Add raisins and/or walnuts, if desired. Spoon batter into
greased pie dish and bake for 30 minutes. Serve warm or at room temperature,
topping slices with whipped cream. —2003 COLLECTORS ISSUE

DUTCH APPLE CAKE
Helen Hunter, Fort Myers, Florida

•----------•

SERVES 6–8.

2 cups McIntosh apples, peeled, cored and diced
1 egg, beaten
1 cup sugar
¾ cup butter or margarine, softened
1 cup flour
1 teaspoon cinnamon
1 teaspoon baking soda
1 teaspoon vanilla

Preheat oven to 350º. Stir together diced apples, egg, sugar and butter. Add flour, cinnamon, baking soda and vanilla. Mix until blended. Bake for 35 to 45 minutes in a greased 9-by-9-inch pan. —2003 COLLECTORS ISSUE

APFELKUCHEN
Ruth Martin, Olmstedville, New York
•----------•

The tradition of passing down recipes brings this unadorned cake to author Bibi Wein from an Adirondack neighbor. Note that ingredients are similar to Dutch and Swedish apple desserts but the technique differs. SERVES 6–8.

½ cup sugar
1 tablespoon butter, plus a little extra for the top
1 egg, room temperature
1 cup all-purpose flour
¼ teaspoon salt
½ teaspoon baking powder
½ cup milk
1 teaspoon vanilla
2–3 apples
2 teaspoons cinnamon

Preheat oven to 350º. Grease and flour a 9-inch baking dish. In a large bowl, cream butter and sugar. Add egg and mix well. Add flour, baking powder, salt and vanilla. Add milk and mix well. Pour batter into baking dish. Peel and core apples, and slice. Arrange apples on top of batter. Sprinkle with cinnamon and dot with butter. Bake for 30 minutes or until toothpick inserted in center of cake comes out clean.

—2003 COLLECTORS ISSUE

SEEK NO MORE

Barbara Wood, Malone, New York

• - - - - - - - - - - •

The yellowish-white flesh of the Seek-No-Further dessert apple (also known as New England Seek-No-Further, Red Winter Pearmain, Signifinger and Westfield) is crisp, tender and juicy with a distinctive aroma and a flavor that's mildly astringent. If you're unable to find this heirloom variety, try Honeycrisp or an apple with a crunchy, juicy flesh. SERVES 4.

4 Seek-No-Further apples
½ cup dark brown sugar
½ stick butter (¼ cup)
1 jigger Grand Marnier
4 scoops vanilla ice cream
1 cup whipped cream
Nutmeg

Wash apples. Slice off tops with stems and set aside. Peel, core and slice apples.
   In medium to large saucepan, cook apples, sugar, butter and Grand Marnier on medium heat for 20 minutes. Pour over ice cream. Cover with a dollop of whipped cream, sprinkle with a grating of nutmeg and cap with the apple top.

—2003 COLLECTORS ISSUE

APPLE-CRANBERRY CRUMB CAKE
Moira Dick, Syracuse, New York

• - - - - - - - - - •

Apples and cranberries are the perfect fall combination. SERVES 12.

1½ cups all-purpose flour
1 cup sugar
½ cup butter or margarine
½ teaspoon cinnamon
½ cup buttermilk
1 egg
½ teaspoon baking soda
1 cup Crispin apples, peeled, cored and diced (1–2 apples)
½ cup dried cranberries (or Craisins)

Preheat oven to 300°. Mix flour, sugar and butter together in a medium bowl until crumbly. Divide mixture into two bowls (approximately 1½ cups each).

In the first bowl, mix in cinnamon and set aside for the topping. In the second bowl, add buttermilk, egg and baking soda. Mix just until smooth. Add apples and cranberries and lightly stir into the batter. Spread batter into a greased 8-inch-square baking pan. Sprinkle cinnamon mixture over the top.

Bake at 300° for 45 minutes or until firm in the middle. —2003 COLLECTORS ISSUE

APPLE-CHOCOLATE-CARAMEL CHEESECAKE
Moira Dick, Syracuse, New York
•----------•

Cheesecake makes any occasion special, particularly when the recipe calls for apples, chocolate and caramel. This presentation is as impressive as the flavor combination. SERVES 8–10.

1½ cups graham cracker crumbs
¾ cup sugar
¼ cup butter, melted

3–4 Crispin apples (4 cups), peeled, cored and sliced
4 cups water
¼ cup lemon juice
1 envelope unflavored gelatin
8 ounces cream cheese
½ cup milk
2 cups heavy cream
12 ounces chocolate chips
¾ cup caramel ice-cream topping
1 cup Skor English Toffee Bits

Preheat oven to 350º.

CRUST:
Combine graham crackers, ¼ cup sugar and butter. Blend well. Press into the base

of a 9-inch springform pan. Bake at 350° for 5 minutes, then let cool.

APPLES:
Bring 4 cups water and lemon juice to a boil in a medium saucepan. Add apples and return to a boil. Drain pan and fill with cold running water, rinsing until cold. Let apple slices drain well while preparing rest of cheesecake.

GANACHE:
Heat 1 cup heavy cream just to a simmer in a heavy saucepan. Remove from heat and whip in chocolate chips until smooth. Set aside.

CHEESECAKE:
Sprinkle gelatin over ¼ cup cold water. Let soften for 5 minutes. Heat gelatin over low heat to dissolve; set aside. Blend cream cheese and ½ cup sugar until smooth. Slowly add milk and gelatin (alternating) while continuing to blend. Chill until mixture starts to set. Whip 1 cup heavy cream to stiff peaks; fold into thickened cream-cheese mixture.

Spread layers as follows: graham crust, a third of cheesecake filling, half of apple slices, caramel ice-cream topping (thin layer), chocolate ganache (thin layer), a third of Skor Toffee Bits. Repeat, ending with cheesecake layer. Fill 2 pastry bags (with writing tips), one with caramel topping and one with chocolate ganache. Make a circle pattern on top of cake. Make one circle of each size of each flavor. Draw a butter knife from outside edge to center of the cake making 16 marks. Sprinkle outside edge and center with toffee bits. Refrigerate 4 to 5 hours or overnight. Remove pan to serve. —2003 COLLECTORS ISSUE

VANILLA CRÈME BRÛLÉE

Chef Robert Borden, Lake Placid, New York

•----------•

Trained by chefs Jacques Torres, of Le Cirque, and Daniel Boulud, of Restaurant Daniel, and at the French Culinary Institute—all in New York City—Rob Borden noted that his mother-in-law, Jeanine Laliberté-Butler, inspired this recipe for a classic French custard. This dish is great served with almond cookies or biscotti and espresso. Borden was the chef at Lake Placid's former Le Bistro Laliberté. SERVES 8.

1 cup dark brown sugar
1 cup whole milk
3 cups heavy cream
1 vanilla bean
1 whole egg
8 egg yolks
1 cup granulated sugar
1 teaspoon vanilla extract

Spread brown sugar on a sheet pan or plate and leave uncovered 2 to 3 hours to remove moisture.

Preheat oven to 250°. Pour cream and milk into a 2-quart saucepan, split the vanilla bean lengthwise, and scrape the seeds into the cream. Over medium heat, scald the cream (do not boil) and set aside.

In a large mixing bowl, whisk the whole egg with the yolks, and then the granulated sugar, in that order, until well blended. Slowly pour the cream mixture over the eggs, stirring (not beating) so the eggs don't scramble. Strain, removing the vanilla seeds, then add the vanilla extract.

Place 8 oval ramekins, 5 inches long by 1 inch deep (4-ounce capacity), in a sheet pan or roasting pan and fill each ¾ full of custard. Place the pan in the middle of the oven and carefully pour hot water around ramekins to halfway up the sides. Bake 30 to 45 minutes, until custard trembles slightly when touched. Cool to room temperature. Custards will keep 3 to 5 days covered and refrigerated.

To finish, pass brown sugar through a sieve held above the custards and lightly dust until each is evenly covered. Clean edges of ramekins and position 4 to 6 inches from broiler element. Remove when topping is light golden brown, 2 to 5 minutes.

—JUNE 1999

APPLE SCHNITZER
Beverly Fickbohm, Cranberry Lake, New York

• - - - - - - - - - - •

These apples are cooked in a schnitzer, a small cast-iron or porcelain-lined dish with a spike in the center, which makes the apples cook from the inside out. Using this method on top of your woodstove, your house will be filled with a wonderful aroma, and you'll have dessert without expending any extra fuel. SERVES 1.

1 Rome Beauty apple
1 tablespoon brown sugar
⅛ teaspoon ground cinnamon
1½ teaspoons butter
Chopped walnuts
Raisins

Wash and core apple. Pare skin from top third of apple and place the apple on the schnitzer, pared end up. For each apple mix together the brown sugar and cinnamon, sprinkle over the top of the apple. Dot with butter, add chopped walnuts and/or raisins to the apple cavity and place on top of woodstove. Cook ½ to 1 hour, until apple is tender but not too soft.

Variation: **Prepare apple as stated above and place in a ceramic baking dish. Bake at 400° for approximately 25 to 35 minutes.** —FEBRUARY 1987

BOILED RAISIN CAKE

Gladys Deloria, Au Sable Forks, New York

•----------•

A mainstay of old lumber camps, this dessert uses ingredients found in any old-time larder. SERVES 8.

1 cup sugar
⅓ cup shortening
1½ cups cold water
1 cup seedless raisins
½ teaspoon nutmeg
½ teaspoon cloves
1 teaspoon cinnamon
1 teaspoon baking soda
2 tablespoons warm water
1¾ cups all-purpose flour
1 teaspoon baking powder

Preheat oven to 350°. In a medium saucepan, place sugar, shortening, cold water, raisins, nutmeg, cloves and cinnamon over medium-high heat and boil for 3 minutes; remove from heat. In a medium bowl, dissolve baking soda in 2 tablespoons warm water; add flour and baking powder. When sugar, shortening and spice mixture is lukewarm mix all ingredients together in bowl.

Place batter in 9-inch-square baking pan and bake for 45 minutes, or until a toothpick inserted in the center comes out clean. This cake can be served plain or with a cream-cheese frosting. —FEBRUARY 1977

CHOCOLATE BREAD PUDDING
Ann Schuyler, Little Falls, New York

•----------•

SERVES 6.

3 cups milk
3 squares unsweetened chocolate
3 slices white bread, broken into bite-size pieces
½ cup sugar
2 eggs
1 teaspoon salt
1 teaspoon vanilla
2 tablespoons butter

Heat milk and chocolate in the top of a double boiler over medium-high heat until chocolate is melted. Turn off heat. Remove ½ cup and add bread to remaining milk and chocolate. In a separate bowl, beat eggs and add reserved ½ cup of milk and chocolate. Add sugar and stir until dissolved. Pour into greased medium casserole, add several small pats of butter on top, and bake for 45 minutes. You may also divide into 6 ramekins and bake for 20 to 25 minutes.

Serve as is, with a side of ice cream or top pudding with the following sugar glaze.

SUGAR GLAZE:
2 tablespoons hot water
¼ teaspoon vanilla
1 cup confectioners' sugar

Stir water with sugar, a few drops at a time. Blend in vanilla and incorporate until smooth. Drizzle over pudding and serve. —WINTER 1976

CHOCOHOLIC PIE
Marcia Twichell, Lake Placid, New York

• - - - - - - - - - - •

According to this recipe's author, "If you would rather take a vacation in Hershey, Pennsylvania, than in Florida, and if you eat M&M's so fast that they never have a chance to melt in your mouth, much less in your hands, then you are a chocoholic." SERVES 6–8.

¼ pound (1 stick) butter, softened
¾ cup confectioners' sugar
3 ounces unsweetened chocolate (3 squares)
2 eggs
1 8-inch baked piecrust
¾ cup heavy cream, whipped
¼ ounce shaved, semisweet chocolate

Melt the unsweetened chocolate in a double boiler over simmering water. When completely melted, cool for 15 minutes. In a large bowl, beat the softened butter for 5 minutes with an electric mixer. Add sugar and beat for 5 minutes. Add eggs, one at a time, until mixture is thick and creamy. Pour into prepared piecrust and refrigerate until firm (2 hours). Top with whipped cream and shaved chocolate.

Note: Double filling ingredients for a 10-inch crust. —WINTER 1975

PIECRUST (FOR ONE DOUBLE-CRUST PIE)
Annette Nielsen, Salem, New York

• - - - - - - - - - - •

EACH PIE SERVES 4–6.

⅔ cup plus 2 tablespoons butter or shortening
2 cups flour
1 teaspoon salt
1 egg, slightly beaten
3 tablespoons cold water (iced)

Sift together flour and salt. Cut shortening into flour until the size of peas. Mix together slightly beaten egg and 2 tablespoons ice water. Stir into flour mixture until moistened, adding more water if needed. Gather dough into a ball, divide in half and flatten each into rounds. Wrap individually in waxed paper or plastic wrap and refrigerate for about an hour. On a lightly floured board, roll pastry out to about an inch larger than pie plate. Ease dough into pie plate and fill, topping with second round of rolled-out dough. —INSPIRED BY "TUPPER LAKE TOURTIÉRE," DECEMBER 2008

MAPLE MOUSSE IN LACE WALNUT BASKETS

Moira Dick, Syracuse, New York

•----------•

This dessert with its elegant presentation offers a lighter option after a hearty meal.
SERVES 8.

BASKETS:
½ **cup butter**
½ **cup corn syrup**
½ **cup brown sugar**
⅔ **cup all-purpose flour**
½ **cup ground walnuts**
Parchment paper

Preheat oven to 350°. In a medium saucepan over medium heat, mix butter, corn syrup and brown sugar. Heat until melted and remove before mixture begins boiling. Stir in flour and nuts; mix well and set aside.

  Cut sheets of parchment paper into 8 8-by-6-inch pieces. Spray each sheet with pan release and place on baking trays. Drop the batter evenly onto each piece of paper. Bake 12 minutes. The cookies should bubble and turn an even brown color. Let cool for 1 minute, then place unformed baskets over inverted soup cups sprayed with pan release. Let cool and harden into shape.

MOUSSE:
¾ **cup maple syrup**
1 envelope Knox unflavored gelatin

3 eggs, separated
2 tablespoons brown sugar
1 cup heavy cream
2 tablespoons Nocello Walnut Liqueur (similar in taste to Frangelico)
Whipped cream (for garnish)
Chopped walnuts (for garnish)

Mix maple syrup and gelatin in a medium saucepan. Let set for 5 minutes until mixture thickens. Heat over medium heat until gelatin dissolves. Remove from heat. Incorporate egg yolks and allow to cool.

In a mixing bowl, beat the egg whites until foamy. Add brown sugar and beat until stiff. In another bowl, beat heavy cream and liqueur until thick. Fold all 3 mixes—gelatin, egg whites and heavy cream—together and chill overnight. Pipe mousse into lace baskets and garnish with whipped cream and chopped walnuts. —APRIL 2002

NORTH COUNTRY BAKLAVA
Annette Nielsen, Salem, New York

• - - - - - - - - - - •

Maple syrup replaces honey in this take on a Middle Eastern tradition. Not quite as sweet as the honey version, the cinnamon and cloves add to the layering of maple and walnut flavors. If you use a dark amber syrup, the distinctive flavor will intensify.
YIELD: ABOUT 36 SMALL PASTRIES.

PASTRY:
1 pound (24 sheets) phyllo dough
2 sticks unsalted butter, melted

SYRUP:
2 cups sugar
1 cup maple syrup
1½ cups water
2 tablespoons lemon juice
2 sticks cinnamon
5 whole cloves

Stir the sugar, maple syrup, water, lemon juice, cinnamon sticks and cloves over low heat until the sugar dissolves, about 5 minutes. Stop stirring and increase the heat to medium, and cook until the mixture is slightly syrupy, about 5 minutes (it will register 225° on a candy thermometer). Discard the cinnamon sticks and whole cloves. Let cool.

FILLING:
1 pound (4 cups) walnuts, finely chopped or coarsely ground
¼ cup sugar
1½ teaspoons ground cinnamon
¼ teaspoon ground cloves

Preheat oven to 350°. Combine all of the filling ingredients in a bowl. With some of the melted butter, grease a 13-by-9-inch baking pan or a 15-by-10-inch jelly-roll pan. Place a sheet of phyllo in the prepared pan and lightly brush with butter. Repeat with 7 more sheets. Spread with half of the filling. Top with 8 more sheets, brushing each with butter. Spread with the remaining nut mixture and top with a layer of 8 sheets, continuing to brush each with butter. Trim any overhanging edges. Using a sharp knife, cut 6 equal lengthwise strips through the top layer of pastry. Make 1½-inch wide diagonal cuts across the strips to form diamond shapes.

Just before baking, lightly sprinkle the top of the pastry with cold water. This inhibits the pastry from curling. Bake for 20 minutes. Reduce heat to 300° and bake until golden brown, about 15 more minutes.

Cut through the scored lines. Drizzle the cooled syrup slowly over the hot baklava and let cool for at least 4 hours. —APRIL 2002

FRUIT FRITTERS
Rena Baker, Willsboro, New York

• - - - - - - - - - - •

The person who submitted this recipe—providing only the initials "L. A."—lived in a red brick farmhouse overlooking Lake Champlain formerly owned by Rena "Mother" Baker. Mother Baker was born in the house and, although she lived in other parts of the Adirondacks, returned to it later in her life. This recipe was found by L. A. in a carefully wrapped bundle in the basement, a treasure of two neatly penned recipe books bearing Rena Baker's name. Included in the packet were also ideas for treating frostbite and blood poisoning, using items like turpentine, lard and flaxseed. SERVES 6.

1 cup flour
1½ teaspoons baking powder
½ teaspoon salt
3 tablespoons confectioners' sugar
⅓ cup milk
1 egg, beaten
2 cups fruit (apple slices, banana, pineapple or pear slices, or combination)
2–3 cups vegetable oil

In a medium bowl, mix dry ingredients. In a smaller bowl, whisk together egg and milk, then add to the dry ingredients. Heat oil in a large frying pan until very hot, but not smoking. You need at least an inch of hot oil for best results. Dip fruit pieces in batter and fry, turning once after a few minutes, until the batter is golden brown. Remove from frypan and drain on paper towels. Sprinkle with confectioners' sugar. Serve hot. —SPRING 1975

BAG PUDDING

James Howard Kunstler, Saratoga Springs, New York

•----------•

In his article "Land of Plenty of Nothing," writer James Howard Kunstler explored the history of regional food, from Native American survival meals to pioneer creations relying on staples like cornmeal, lard and maple sweetening. Hoptoad (almost identical to Italian polenta) and suppawn (cornmeal boiled in milk for breakfast) were part of a settler's diet, augmented in the 1800s by the potato. Boiled dinners were commonplace, using pickled meats and hardy vegetables, slow cooked on top of a woodstove, and desserts like the one below became popular using the water from the savory boiled dishes.

Small cloth sack
Cornmeal
Wheat flour
Milk
Sugar
Raisins

Take a small cloth sack (such as the type salt was sold in) and fill with a dough made of equal quantities of cornmeal, wheat flour and milk. Add sugar, to taste, and a handful of raisins. Drop into a simmering pot of liquor (stock) from a boiled dinner for half an hour.

Note: **The advantage to this dish was clearly convenience—a dessert that requires little time and no extra utensils. The drawback—a dessert that potentially smells like corned beef and cabbage.** —FEBRUARY 1990

SUET PUDDING

Jayne Hahne, Ray Brook, New York

•----------•

Adirondack grandmothers knew how to make suet pudding, but they didn't see fit to pass the recipe along. Suet is the solid white fat found around the loins and kidneys of beef, sheep and other animals. Many British recipes employ suet to add richness to mincemeat, puddings and pastries. SERVES 6–8.

2½ cups flour
½ teaspoon salt
½ teaspoon cinnamon
1 teaspoon baking soda
1 cup raisins
½ cup chopped nuts
1 cup milk
1 cup molasses
1 cup chopped suet (beef)

Sift flour, salt, cinnamon and baking soda together and thoroughly mix in raisins, nuts, milk, molasses and suet. Suet should be fresh and finely chopped or ground. Pour mixture into greased and floured mold (1½ quart or slightly larger), cover tightly with aluminum foil and place on a trivet in large container of boiling water. Water should come about halfway up the sides of the mold.

Cover and steam for 3 hours over medium heat; steam should circulate freely around mold. Remove from heat, unmold and serve with whipped cream or the following hard sauce or flambé with brandy.

HARD SAUCE:
½ cup butter, softened
1½ cups confectioners' sugar
2 teaspoons vanilla

Cream the butter with a handheld mixer. Blend in sugar and vanilla. Serve over the warm pudding. —WINTER 1974

TARTE AU SUCRE
Barbara Labbé Getty, Old Forge, New York

• - - - - - - - - - - •

Maple syrup adds another regional layer to this ultra-rich traditional French-Canadian sugar pie. SERVES 8.

2 beaten eggs
2 tablespoons flour
1 cup light or dark brown sugar
1 cup maple syrup
2 tablespoons melted butter

Mix all together. Pour into uncooked pie shell. Bake at 375° for 30 minutes. Allow to cool before serving. —OCTOBER 2009

INDEX